CREATIVE
WOK
COOKING

Ethel Graham and Richard Ahrens

WEATHERVANE
BOOKS

PICTURE CREDITS

The following pictures were provided through the
courtesy of Transworld Feature Syndicate, Inc.:

Syndication International: pp. 4 11 23 30
46 61 69 89 92 99 113 133

Scoop: pp. 65 71 72 73 77

Sungravure Syndication: p. 25

We would also like to thank La Choy Food
Products (A Division of Beatrice Foods Co.)
for allowing us to use the pictures on the following pages: 26 27 28 94 95

Contents

Introduction: Creative Wok Cookery   5

Chapter 1 Basic Ingredients   7

Chapter 2 Stir-Frying   10

      Beef   13

      Chicken   31

      Pork   47

      Szechwan   53

      Shrimp and Lobster   57

      Vegetables and Rice   63

Chapter 3 Steaming   71

Chapter 4 Deep-Frying   83

      Tempura   84

      Deep-Fried Dishes with Sauces   88

      Egg Rolls   96

      Other   103

Chapter 5 Hot-Pot Cookery   105

Chapter 6 Red-Stewing   108

Chapter 7 Soups   111

Chapter 8 Other Recipes   121

Chapter 9 Hors d'Oeuvres   135

Chapter 10 Desserts   139

Index   142

*(left to right) a chinese buffet for eight with easy to prepare
dishes and an exotic fruit dessert:
sweet-and-sour shrimp
fried rice with ham
pork and spring onions
shredded chicken with almonds
mixed vegetables chinese style
beef with chow mein noodles
crispy pancake rolls with pork
mandarin fruit*

4

introduction

creative wok cookery

The art of Chinese cookery is a meticulous one, and in some ways it is complex. However, there is an essential logic and simplicity about its principles, and it can be mastered quite easily by those with a little patience and a great love for food. Even a beginner can produce authentic dishes without difficulty in an ordinary kitchen, using no more than ordinary skills.

The people of China are many in number, and neither they nor their country can be described as rich. Because China is not rich, meats such as pork, liver, beef, duck, chicken, and lamb are sold by the ounce and used sparingly in Chinese cooking. The diet that has evolved over the course of centuries is heavily reliant on such foods as rice, noodles, and vegetables. Indeed, the Chinese have elevated vegetable cookery to a high art. The small amount of meat that is used is usually exquisitely flavored to achieve very delicate nuances. Such nuances of flavor and certain dishes have come to be associated with four different areas in China itself:

1) Northern or Peking Area—The staple food here is not rice but wheat flour, from which are made many noodle dishes, steamed bread, and dumplings. Northern food generally tends to be lighter than that of other provinces. Barbequed meat and hot-pot cookery are predominant. The most famous Northern delicacy is Peking Duck. Traditionally, the duck's carcass is first made fairly airtight by tying up the neck opening, and then the skin is inflated away from the flesh until it is taut. Then it is roasted slowly until the thick, fat skin becomes crisp and golden in color. This crackled skin is the choice part of the dish, though the flesh beneath is also eaten. The skin, together with a piece of the meat, a spring onion, and a thick, sweet sauce, is served as a sandwich, made either by folding over a pancake or with two flaps of steamed bread. The combined tastes and textures give an experience that will long be remembered as one of life's real pleasures.

2) Coastal, Shanghai, or Fukien Area—More soy sauce and sugar are used in cooking seafood and soups, and beef, pork, and chicken dishes are made by stewing in soy sauce. There are gently spiced concoctions of meat, chicken, duck, and seafood with, of course, lots of vegetables. The celebrated dishes of Shanghai in the north include Bird's-Nest Soup and a wide range of seafood. Fukien in the south produces the best soy sauce, and there is a great deal of stewing in this sauce. This is called "red-cooking" because of the color the sauce imparts. The seafood is excellent, and the soups are clear and light. Thin dough wrappers, called Soft Spring Rolls, are stuffed with a great variety of mixtures of several meats and vegetables.

3) Inland or Szechwan Area—This is the country of Szechwan pepper, called fagara. This is different from the pepper we know. It has a peculiar delayed reaction. At first it seems to have no flavor at all, and then there is a strong and hot aftertaste which can numb the mouth of the novice. Vigor and zest characterize the dishes from this area. Small red chilies or Szechwan peppers are used liberally for seasoning, and they are so smolderingly hot that they make the pepper seem bland in comparison. Characteristic dishes are Szechwan Beef, Szechwan Chicken (Kang Pao Chicken), Twice-Cooked Szechwan Pork and Szechwan Duck (Peking Duck's cousin). The latter dish is spiced with pepper and deep-fried after steaming to remove the fat. The meat is so tender it falls apart at a touch, and even the bones are tender enough to chew and digest.

4) Southern or Canton Area—The cooking is subtle and the least greasy of all the regional styles. The cooks excel in stir-frying. Because Chinese from this area were the first to migrate to the United States in large numbers in the mid-nineteenth century, dishes from this area are best-known to Americans. Egg Rolls, Egg Foo Young, Barbecued Pork, Shark's-Fin Soup, and Turtle Soup are from this area. The cuisine tends to be more costly than the others because the cooks use highly concentrated chicken broth as the basis of their soups and general cooking.

5

Cantonese cooking uses a lighter-colored soy sauce that does not detract from the natural flavors of the ingredients. Such a sauce is available in Oriental-food stores.

chinese cooking utensils

An old Chinese proverb says, "To have the job well done, first sharpen the tools." Needless to say, you cannot sharpen tools that you don't own. The first requirement for successful Chinese cooking is to have the correct tools for the job:

1) The wok—This is the most versatile of all kitchen tools. It should win the blue ribbon in any kitchenware competition. Traditionally, woks were made of cast iron, but today they are also made of other metals. Some people will say that an ordinary frying pan is an acceptable substitute for the wok. Don't believe them. The conical shape of the wok makes it ideal for deep-frying, as it requires less oil than a flat-bottomed frying pan. This greater depth gives more frying surface, which uses less fuel, and the greater capacity at the upper end makes overflowing unlikely as more food is added. The wok will stand very high heat. The depth of the wok allows cooking of large fish that would not fit a traditional frying pan. Tilting a wok allows you to make an omelet of almost any size. It makes an excellent steamer with the addition of a rack or bamboo steamers. If your wok is not electric, it is critical that the wok be in direct contact with the heat source. A ring is supplied with the wok for use with gas and electric stoves. The wide end of the ring is placed directly around a gas burner. This ring is inverted so the smaller end sits on the chrome ring around the electric unit, and the wok sits in the larger end. Eventually, heat will discolor the chrome rim on the stove somewhat.

2) Bamboo steamers—These are a series of circular, stackable, interlocking bamboo trays that can be placed in the wok pan. A small amount of water is heated in the bottom of the wok, and the steam cooks the tray contents evenly. The water may be added to by pouring more down the inside face of the wok. The trays have slotted bottoms so that steam can rise from the bottom to the top and little heat is wasted. The rising steam is sealed in by the tight fitting between the bottom tray and the sides of the wok pan. Five to 15 minutes are needed for quick steaming. Slow steaming takes about 40 minutes to an hour. These steamers deteriorate with long use and are expensive. A rack placed in the wok above the water level is possibly a good alternative. A single layer of cheesecloth placed over the rack will prevent food from adhering to it.

3) Chinese cleavers—There are two basic types: a heavy chopper, and a thinner slicer and chopper. The Chinese cook uses the cleaver on a chopping block generally made from the cross section of a tree trunk. With a cleaver, food can be cubed, sliced, chopped, minced, or shredded to any size. A Chinese cleaver may look like a deadly weapon, but the Chinese have developed a safe technique for handling it. Grasp the blade between thumb and forefinger just forward of the handle and let the remaining fingers fall naturally along the side of the blade. Hold the object to be cut with your fingers tucked under, and grip it with the fingertips. Cut carefully, with the flat of the blade held against the knuckles as a guide. Safety is enhanced if the cleaver is lifted only a little.

4) Brass strainers—These are used to drain deep-fried food. They have bamboo handles to prevent the transmission of heat.

5) Ladles and spatulas—These are used to toss and turn foods during stir-frying and for the same uses as in American cooking.

6) Bamboo wok scrubber—This inexpensive item resembles a small whisk broom but is made of narrow strips of bamboo for cleaning the wok.

The wok should be seasoned before use by rubbing the inside surface thoroughly with cooking oil, heating over low heat, and continuing to rub with oil to close the microscopic pores in the metal. Clean with soap and water and a nonabrasive scrubber, such as the bamboo wok scrubber, after each use. Non-sticking oils made with lecithin are available for periodic reseasoning.

chapter 1

basic ingredients

Many ingredients used in Oriental wok cookery are available in supermarkets; others may be obtained from Oriental-food stores. Some foods can be grown in a home garden or in a large pot on an apartment balcony. Give great care to ingredient selection, as cooking rarely improves a poor-quality selection.

Broth: If a recipe calls for stock or broth, a good chicken broth should be used. A bouillon cube dissolved in water makes a poor substitute because it is salty and lacks the rich, characteristic flavor of a good broth. Chicken broth may be purchased canned but this seems quite unnecessary, as it is easily prepared from the bones and skin left from boned and skinned chicken used in nearly all stir-fried chicken dishes. Place the bones and skins in a saucepan, add 2 cups of water for every cup of bones, and simmer covered for about 2 hours. Strain the fragrant broth into a jar; cover and refrigerate it. Do not add salt. The broth will keep about a week — longer if frozen in plastic containers. Glass jars crack in the freezer. Four boned chicken-breast halves provide about 2 cups of broth, sufficient for two or three stir-fried dishes or the basis for soup to serve four. Before using the broth, remove the layer of congealed fat from the surface. Broth often gels when chilled, as gelatin leaches out of the bones during simmering. It will reliquify when heated.

Oil: Vegetable oil must be used whenever high-temperature frying is done. Stir-frying requires temperatures close to 375°F. Avoid butter, which burns at 225°F, and hydrogenated shortening, which begins to smoke at 350°F. Oil will not smoke or decompose unless it is overheated to about 450°F.

Cornstarch: Cornstarch is used as the thickening agent in sauces and gravies. It must always be dispersed in a cold liquid ingredient or in a little water and be given a quick stir before adding it to hot ingredients. Otherwise, the cornstarch particles tend to settle to the bottom of cold liquids and clump together when heated. Lumps in the gravy are a result. Always stir a cornstarch mixture as it is heated. This also will prevent lumps.

vegetables

Vegetables should always be garden-fresh for sweetness and crispness. If you happen to have a small home garden where you can grow several vegetables, Oriental wok cookery is a must! No other cooking method will retain so much of the sweet flavor and crispy texture of freshly grown pea pods, green peppers, carrots, and others. Vegetables purchased in supermarkets or from roadside stands must be used as quickly as possible. Canned and frozen vegetables can be used, but processing always softens their texture.

Bamboo shoots: Shoots of the tropical bamboo. These are usually purchased canned from supermarkets and are valuable for their interesting texture. They will keep 1 to 2 weeks stored in water in a covered jar in the refrigerator. Change the water in the jar each day.

Bean curd: Cakes of precipitated soybean protein. These are available in Oriental-food stores and cubed for addition to stir-fried dishes and soups. They keep for 1 to 2 weeks refrigerated in a covered jar with fresh water. Change the water daily.

Bean sprouts: Sprouts of the mung bean. These are available canned in supermarkets, but we prefer to grow our own. Fresh sprouts are crunchy and far less expensive. A garden and soil are not necessary. Purchase the small, green, dried mung beans at a health or natural-food store. They can be sprouted and ready for use in 3 to 4 days.

1. Place 2 to 3 tablespoons of mung beans in a pint-size or larger jar. Cover the beans with 2 cups of water and soak overnight.

2. In the morning drain off the water and cover the top of the jar with 1 layer of cheesecloth fastened with a rubber band.

3. Place the jar in a dark cabinet at room temperature for 3 to 4 days. (If the jar is left out in the room, green leaves form rather than long sprouts.)

4. Rinse the beans 3 times a day during this storage time by adding water and draining well directly through the cheesecloth cover.

5. After 3 days, the sprouts will be 1 to 2 inches long. Cover the jar with a lid. Refrigerate and use within several days. Chilling stops their growth. Serve just barely heated with soy sauce, or use them in stir-fried dishes or omelets.

7

Chinese mustard cabbage: Dark-green, stalky cabbage with a bitter flavor. It is used in stir-fried dishes and soups. It is available in Oriental-food stores. It keeps nearly a week in the refrigerator. It is also available pickled.

Garlic: Available in supermarkets. The cloves are never left whole in the completed dish, but are removed after imparting a flavor to the oil. It may also be grated or minced and used either in a marinade or as a flavoring ingredient.

Fresh ginger root: A 3- to 5-inch brown root available in most supermarkets. It must be used for Oriental wok cookery! Powdered ginger is a poor substitute. Only if absolutely necessary use ¼ teaspoon of powdered ginger for 1 teaspoon of grated ginger root. It is usually grated, but slices may be used. Never leave a slice in the completed dish, as the flavor is strong and slightly hot. It keeps a month or longer if wrapped tightly and refrigerated.

Chinese dried black mushrooms: Available in cellophane bags in Oriental-food stores. They are rather expensive, so only a few are used in a recipe. They give an interesting color and texture to stir-fried dishes. Soak them in warm water for 20 to 30 minutes, remove the stems, and slice. Dried, they will keep months in a covered jar.

Mushrooms: Available fresh or canned in supermarkets. Fresh mushrooms are superior, as they are not water-logged. If canned mushrooms are used, they are heated or stir-fried for a shorter period of time than the fresh, and they tend to spatter.

Scallions: Also known as spring onions. They are available in supermarkets. They keep a week or two covered in the refrigerator. Use the green tops as well as the root bulbs.

Snow pea pods: Grow your own! A 6-ounce frozen package from the supermarket is expensive, costing four or five times the price of other vegetables. These pods are marvelous in stir-fried dishes and are one ingredient you won't want to omit. Snow pea pod seeds are available now from all major seed companies by mail order. In Maryland we plant them in a row every 4 inches in early April. By early June an 8-foot row in poor soil yields a gallon of pods, enough for many stir-fried dishes. (Try them in Moo Goo Gai Pan!) Then the small vines are pulled up for a crop of cucumbers. Snow pea pods need to be stringed. Pull off the strings that run down either side of the

pod before cooking them. Stir-fry only until their green color intensifies and they are still crisp.

Chinese cabbage (bok choy): Has stalks and dark-green leaves. It is used in stir-fried dishes and soups. It is available in Oriental-food stores and some supermarkets. It keeps about a week in the refrigerator, covered.

Chinese celery cabbage (sin choy): Resembles both celery and white cabbage, with its tightly packed stalks. It is available in most supermarkets. Covered, it keeps about a week in the refrigerator. It is prepared by slicing across the stalks.

Water chestnuts: Small, white, crunchy bulbs available canned in supermarkets. Refrigerate them in water in a covered jar. They keep nearly a month if the water in the jar is changed daily. We like to substitute Jerusalem artichoke roots when they are available during the winter months. We also grow these in our garden and harvest the roots after the plant dies back in the fall. Leave the unused roots in the ground and dig them up as needed. The Jerusalem artichoke is a member of the sunflower family.

Other fresh vegetables commonly used: Green and red bell peppers; tomatoes, peeled; carrots; green beans; asparagus; and celery.

Rice: Many types of rice are available at supermarkets. Long-, short-, and medium-grain rices refer to the size of the kernel. Generally, the long-grain rices are least sticky, and many Oriental restaurants use this type for plain, boiled rice and fried rice. The shorter-grain rices tend to stick together after cooking.

Enriched or polished rice has had the nutritious bran layer and germ removed by milling. Most of the vitamins and almost half of the minerals are removed. Thiamine, niacin, and iron are then added to the rice as a coating to replace partially some of the lost minerals and vitamins. This type of rice keeps well and cooks in 15 to 25 minutes, depending on the kernel size.

Quick-cooking or instant rice is precooked, enriched rice. The cost is more per serving.

Converted or parboiled rice is partially steamed under pressure before the bran layer and germ are removed by milling. This forces many of the nutrients into the endosperm, and the nutritive value of the milled kernel is similar to that of the whole grain.

Brown or whole-grain rice is the most nutritious

rice because none of the vitamins and minerals have been removed by milling. Its flavor may deteriorate during long storage if the oils in the germ become rancid. Its cooking time is about twice as long as the enriched rice because the cooking water must penetrate the bran layer before it can gelatinize and soften the starch in the endosperm. However, we add the amount of water we would use for cooking to the rice about 2 to 3 hours before a meal. The bran absorbs some of the water, and the cooking time is cut in half. This saves time and fuel! We recommend this type of rice because of its nutritive value, nutty flavor, and the presence of fiber in the brain.

meat, fish, and poultry

Beef: Flank steak, top of the round, and chuck blade steaks are most often sliced or cubed for stir-frying. More tender cuts from the rib, loin, and sirloin can be used but are an unnecessary expense. Brisket and shank meat should be used for stewing. They are not sufficiently tender for use in stir-fried dishes.

Pork: All cuts are used, as there is little variation in tenderness. Shoulder cuts and cuts from the leg are often good buys if they are lean.

Chicken: Breast meat is best for stir-fried dishes. Other parts are reserved for stewing. The breast meat is easily removed from the bone by inserting a sharp knife along the breastbone and running it close against the ribs. Reserve the skin and bones for broth. Skin and bones from two whole breasts will yield 2 to 3 cups of broth for use in several stir-fry recipes or as a basis for soups.

Fish: Fresh fish is preferred, and steaming is usually the preferred cooking method. Once fish has been frozen, it loses its creamy texture and the flesh toughens and becomes dry when cooked.

Shellfish and mollusks: Shrimps, clams, oysters, lobsters, and abalones are used. They are available fresh, canned, or salted and dried. Purchase them at supermarkets. Abalone is available from Oriental-food stores either canned or dried.

other ingredients, seasonings, and sauces

Black bean sauce: Made from fermented black beans, sugar, and flavorings. It is available canned in Oriental-food stores. It keeps refrigerated in a covered jar for up to a year.   Refrigerated and covered, they keep about 6 months.

Fermented black beans (dow see): Available canned or in plastic bags from Oriental-food stores. Strongly flavored and salty, these are usually rinsed, mashed, and heated in oil with garlic. They are used in Lobster Cantonese and Shrimp with Lobster Sauce.

Bird's Nest: Pieces of the gelatinous substance Asian swiftlets use to coat their nuts. It is used mainly in soups. It is available in packages in Oriental-food stores. No refrigeration is needed.

Chili paste: Hot paste made of chili peppers used in Szechwan cooking. Tabasco sauce in small quantities may be substituted. It keeps well in the refrigerator. It is available in jars from Oriental-food store.

Five-spices(s) powder: Used in red-stewing, and in some pork and chicken dishes. It contains fennel, cloves, cinnamon, anise, and Szechwan pepper. It has a hot cinnamon-licorice flavor. It is available from Oriental-food stores and some gourmet shops.

Glutinous rice: A small-grained rice that swells to resemble pearls when steamed. It is available from Oriental-food stores. Do not purchase this as a substitute for long- or short-grained rice. It is used in few recipes.

Hoisin sauce: Thick reddish-brown sauce made of soybeans, garlic, flour, salt, sugar, and chili. It is unique, deliciously hot and sweet. There is no substitute! It is delicious with chicken. It is available from Oriental-food stores in cans. Refrigerate in a jar after opening. It keeps for a year.

Lychees (litchis): Unusual 2-inch fruit sold canned in Oriental-food stores. It is good in stir-fried dishes and with other fruits as a dessert.

Nuts: Cashews are good with beef or chicken, walnuts with beef, and almonds with chicken. Peanuts may be used as a substitute. Never overcook nuts or they soften. Refrigerate shelled nuts to prevent rancidity.

Oyster sauce: Thick, brown sauce made from oysters, soybeans, and salt. It is used as an ingredient or as a dip. It is sold bottled in some supermarkets and in Oriental-food stores. Refrigerate after opening. It keeps for 1 year.

Red dates: Shiny, dried red dates are available in Oriental-food stores. They give a sweet flavor to stews, soups, and dishes cooked for long periods of time. They keep indefinitely in a covered jar.

chapter 2

stir-frying
mastering the technique of stir-frying

Stir-frying is the Chinese technique of continuous stirring, turning, and light tossing of foods one at a time in hot oil in a wok. When one food is heated through, it is pushed up the sloping sides, where it will remain warm while the other foods are stir-fried. When each food has been stir-fried, all are recombined, a sauce is added, and the dish is served at once. Foods are cooked rapidly in only one utensil with only one source of heat, conserving energy. Stir-fried vegetables cook quickly and retain many of their water-soluble vitamins and mineral salts. These ordinarily leach out into cooking water and are discarded. Stir-fried meats also cook quickly and remain tender.

Sesame Oil: Too expensive to use for frying, it is used in small amounts to flavor food after cooking. It resembles peanuts in flavor. It is available bottled from Oriental-food stores. Store in a cool, dark area to prevent rancidity.

Soy sauce: In supermarkets two types are offered—domestic, and imported Japanese. Purchase the imported Japanese type. It has a better flavor, with no burned aftertaste. In Oriental-food stores several types are available—light soy sauce is used mainly for dipping, dark as an ingredient, and thick as a dark coloring agent. The dark sauce contains molasses.

Star anise: A licorice-flavored spice available from Oriental-food stores. It resembles an 8-pointed star. It is used in red-stewing and in some poultry dishes.

Szechwan pepper: Available as whole peppercorns in Oriental-food stores. It must be crushed or ground. It is very hot!

Wines: A good table variety of dry sherry is combined with soy sauce in most beef stir-fry recipes—a flavorful combination! A good table variety of a dry white wine is used in chicken and seafood dishes.

Cooking temperatures. An electric wok is set at 375°F for stir-frying. On the electric and gas stoves where the wok is set in a ring over the electric unit or gas flame, the temperature is kept hot enough to cook foods quickly without burning. Regulate the controls between high and medium heat. An electric frypan or a skillet may be substituted for a wok. These have a larger cooking surface area, and foods will cook more rapidly. Foods cannot be pushed away from the heat source up sloping sides. Therefore, simply remove each food from the skillet to a platter as it is stir-fried. Return everything before the gravy or sauce is added.

cutting and slicing

Proper cutting and slicing are important steps in preparing foods for stir-frying. Cutting pieces into bite-sizes enables the Chinese to eat with chopsticks and omit knives and forks. It also decreases cooking time by increasing the amount of surface area exposed to the heat. In addition, it permits greater absorption of sauces and seasonings by the food and increases tenderness.

All pieces of meat and vegetables used in one recipe are cut into similar shapes and sizes. If a vegetable is cubed, the meat is cut into cubes of similar size and shape. If vegetables are cut into thin slices, the meat in that dish is likewise cut into thin slices.

methods of cutting

Straight slicing: Used for meats and fleshy vegetables such as bamboo shoots, mushrooms, and water chestnuts. Cuts are made with the knife perpendicular to the board.

Diagonal slicing: Used for firm, stringy, stalky vegetables such as carrots, celery, asparagus, and celery cabbage. The knife is held on a slant as it cuts through the food. Diagonally cut celery is very attractive. This is used frequently to cut flank steak against the grain and increase its tenderness.

Roll-slicing: Used for cylindrical vegetables such as carrots and asparagus. The knife is held on a slant and the vegetable is rolled a quarter turn in one direction after each cut.

Shredding: Used for meats and stalky vegetables. Food is cut into lengthwise slices which are stacked and cut lengthwise again into matchstick-size pieces.

Cubing: Used for meats, green peppers, and onions. Food is cut into bite-size squares, ½ to ¾ inch in size.

Mincing: Food is cut into as small pieces as possible.

how to prepare stir-fried dishes

The key to preparing stir-fried dishes is in knowing the order in which foods are seasoned and added to the pan.

Pork and beef are usually marinated for 20 to 30 minutes while the vegetables are being prepared. The marinade may consist of any one or all of the following: soy sauce; a little sugar, not to sweeten but to bring out the flavor of the soy; dry sherry; grated or crushed garlic; and grated fresh ginger root. This procedure gives the meat a lightly salted, good soy flavor. The meat may be left unmarinated, however. These seasonings are then added to the gravy. The meat will be mild and the dark-colored gravy will impart a rich flavor to the dish. You may also compromise and marinate the meat in a little sauce and add the remainder to the gravy.

Chicken, shrimps, and lobster usually are not marinated except perhaps in a little white wine, egg white, and cornstarch to give them a smooth surface when fried.

To begin the stir-fried dish, heat about 2 tablespoons of vegetable oil in the bottom of the wok and swirl it up the sides a bit. A slice of fresh ginger root and a clove of garlic may be browned in the oil to flavor it. These must be removed and discarded so the diner does not bite into one of these strongly flavored pieces as he is enjoying the dish. No ginger root or garlic is added to the marinade or grated as an ingredient if it has flavored the oil.

If unroasted nuts are to be used, they are stir-fried in the heated oil first and then completely removed from the pan. These will not stay in place if pushed up the sides. They are returned to the dish during the last moments of cooking.

Next, the fresh vegetables are stir-fried. Each is cooked for only a minute or two or just until the color intensifies and the vegetable is hot and tender, but still crisp. Some vegetables, such as roll-cut carrots, may require partial boiling first or they will overcook on the outside in the oil before the interior is warm. The fleshiest vegetable requiring the longest heating is stir-fried first. It is pushed up the sides to keep warm, and another vegetable is stir-fried. This is then pushed up the sides, and the most tender vegetables are stir-fried last. If a skillet is used, each vegetable must be removed from the pan as it is cooked, to prevent overheating.

Chicken, beef, lobster, and shrimps are always stir-fried after the vegetables, as over-cooked meats lose tenderness and moisture. Pork is always stir-fried before the vegetables and then pushed up the sides to be sure it is well-cooked. Chicken and beef require only 3 to 4 minutes; lobster and shrimps require only 1 or 2.

The vegetables and meat are then recombined in the wok. A sauce made of meat stock, cornstarch in cold water, and possibly some seasonings or wine is stirred together and added all at once. Everything is heated just until the gravy boils and becomes clear and thickened. Vegetables must remain crisp.

vegetables that have been sliced or shredded in preparation for stir-frying

In dry-cooked dishes no cornstarch gravy is added. Some cornstarch may be added to the meat marinade. A mixture of bean sauce, hoisin sauce, and perhaps some hot seasonings is stirred into the dish as a final step. These dishes are usually strongly flavored. Szechwan stir-fried dishes are an example of the dry-cooking technique.

Just before the dish is served, the nuts are added. They must never be cooked in the gravy for long periods of time or they will lose their crispness and become like beans in texture. The nuts may be sprinkled over the dish when it is placed on a serving platter and not be heated at all with the other ingredients.

A summary of stir-frying steps:

1. Brown nuts in oil. Remove.
2. Stir-fry pork, if used. Push up the sides.
3. Stir-fry each vegetable. Push up the sides.
4. Stir-fry beef, chicken, and seafood last.
5. Return the vegetables to the meat.
6. Add gravy or sauces. Heat until thick.
7. Add nuts.

About the seasonings and gravy:

1. Garlic and ginger left whole to flavor a dish must be removed and discarded. Grated, they remain as an ingredient.

2. Sauces, seasonings, and wine are used as a marinade if the meat is to have a strong flavor. They are used in the gravy if a dark, richly flavored gravy is desired.

3. A gravy may be omitted, with seasonings and sauces added at the end to coat the dish.

Some suggested stir-frying times

Bean sprouts 1 to 2 minutes
Celery cabbage 2 to 3 minutes
Green pepper cubes 1 to 2 minutes
Meats 3 to 4 minutes
Nuts 1 to 2 minutes
Sliced celery 1 to 2 minutes
Snow pea pods 1 to 2 minutes

how to cook creatively with the wok

Any combination of nuts, meats, and vegetables may be selected if the above steps are followed. In the United States 1 pound of meat is used with 2 to 4 cups of prepared vegetables. A

proportion of 1 tablespoon of cornstarch to ½ cup of liquid is used with these amounts as a gravy. You may wish to add more of each to have more gravy. Two to 4 tablespoons of sauces (soy sauce, sherry, black bean sauce, hoisin sauce, etc.) are used in any desired proportion for flavoring.

Every effort should be made to obtain or grow fresh vegetables, as canned or frozen ones can never be crisp.

A trip to an Oriental-food store for those ingredients not available in the supermarket is interesting for the entire family. Fresh ginger root, black bean sauce, fermented black beans, hoisin sauce, chili paste, scallions, Japanese soy sauce, and garlic, you'll surely want to try. Some of these can be obtained through mail-order sources. Do try to obtain hoisin sauce!

what to serve and how much

In many American homes help is not available at mealtimes, and every stir-fried dish must be served immediately after cooking is completed. None can be successfully kept warm while another is prepared. Therefore, unless two members of a family enjoy cooking together, plan to serve only one stir-fried dish at a meal, with rice or noodles and a salad and light dessert. Barbequed Spareribs or Chicken Wings with Oyster Sauce are possible additions to a meal, as they involve no last-moment preparation.

If you wish to serve more than one stir-fried dish, select two or three that complement one another. Vary the main meat and use a highly seasoned dish with a milder one. Have all the ingredients for a second dish prepared—the vegetables chopped, sauces combined, etc., before preparing the first one. Cook the second dish after the first has been eaten and enjoyed. Guests enjoy watching this process if you have an electric wok to bring to the table.

One pound of meat is satisfactory for four persons, and the stir-fried dishes in this book serve four. If more are to be served, make more of one recipe or prepare additional recipes, allowing a total of 4 ounces of meat per person.

On occasion we like to substitute for the rice a mid-Eastern dish made of bulgar (toasted cracked wheat) known as Tabbuleh. The recipe is on the box found in the gourmet section at the supermarket.

beef

The following two recipes are versions of a popular dish, Green Pepper Steak, served in most Chinese restaurants.

In Version 1 the beef is marinated in soy sauce before it is stir-fried. No soy sauce is added to the gravy. This method gives the beef a salty, soy sauce flavor, and the gravy is mild.

In Version 2 the beef is not marinated, and the soy sauce is added to the gravy instead. In this version the meat is mild, but the gravy is very flavorful. Try both versions to determine which method seems best. Recipes in this book use either method, and you may change them to suit your tastes. If marination is not desired, simply add the marination ingredients to the gravy at the end. If the recipe does not call for marination but does contain soy sauce and other seasonings in the gravy, omit these from the gravy and use them for marinating the meat.

green pepper steak (version 1)

Yield: 4 servings

1 pound flank steak, thinly sliced diagonally across grain with knife titled at a 45° angle to the cutting board
3 tablespoons soy sauce
¼ teaspoon sugar
2 tablespoons vegetable oil
1 or 2 green peppers, cut into ¼-inch strips
2 tablespoons cornstarch in 2 tablespoons cold water
1 cup chicken broth or water
2 or 3 firm tomatoes, cut into wedges (peeled, if desired)

Marinate the steak in the soy sauce and sugar for 20 to 30 minutes. Heat oil in the wok and stir-fry the green peppers 1 to 2 minutes or until their green color brightens. Push aside. Stir-fry steak 3 to 4 minutes. Return the green peppers to the steak in the wok. Add the cornstarch mixture and broth to the steak and peppers. Add the tomato wedges and heat, stirring gently, until the sauce is thickened and clear and the tomatoes are heated through. Serve at once with rice.

green pepper steak (version 2)

Yield: 4 servings

2 tablespoons vegetable oil
1 or 2 green peppers, cut into ¼-inch strips
1 pound flank steak, thinly sliced directly across the grain with the knife tilted at a 45° angle to the cutting board
2 tablespoons cornstarch in 2 tablespoons cold water
1 cup chicken broth or water
3 tablespoons soy sauce (more, if desired)
2 or 3 firm tomatoes, cut into wedges (peeled, if desired)

Heat oil in the wok and stir-fry the green peppers 1 to 2 minutes or until their green color brightens. Push aside. Stir-fry the steak 3 to 4 minutes. Return the green peppers to the steak in the wok. Stir the cornstarch mixture, broth, and soy sauce into the steak and peppers. Add the tomato wedges and continue heating until the sauce is thickened and clear and the tomatoes are heated through. Serve at once with rice.

14

beef with snow pea pods and water chestnuts

In this recipe half of the seasoning is added to the beef and used as a marinade. The remaining half of the sauces is added to the gravy. They may, however, be combined and used entirely either as a marinade or as an addition to the gravy.

Yield: 4 servings

1 tablespoon soy sauce
1 tablespoon dry sherry
1 pound beef (top of the round), sliced very thin
2 tablespoons vegetable oil
12 to 16 snow pea pods, strings removed

6 to 8 water chestnuts, sliced
½ cup chicken broth or stock
1 tablespoon soy sauce
1 tablespoon dry sherry
1 tablespoon cornstarch in 2 tablespoons cold water
Walnuts (optional)

Combine 1 tablespoon soy sauce and 1 tablespoon dry sherry in a small bowl. Add sliced beef and let stand 20 to 30 minutes. Heat oil in wok and stir-fry the pea pods 1 to 2 minutes or just until their green color brightens. Push aside. Stir-fry the water chestnuts 1 minute. Push aside. Stir-fry the beef 3 to 4 minutes. Return the pea pods and water chestnuts to the beef in the wok. Add the broth, remaining 1 tablespoon soy sauce, remaining 1 tablespoon dry sherry, and the cornstarch mixture. Heat until the sauce boils and is thickened and clear. Garnish with walnuts if you wish. Serve at once with rice.

beef with asparagus and hoisin sauce

Yield: 4 servings

1 tablespoon soy sauce
1 tablespoon dry sherry
1 teaspoon cornstarch
1 teaspoon grated garlic
1 pound flank steak, thinly sliced with the knife held at 45° angle to the board

2 tablespoons vegetable oil
2 scallions, cut into ¼-inch diagonal slices
1 pound asparagus, cut diagonally into ¼-inch slices
3 tablespoons hoisin sauce
½ cup roasted peanuts

Combine the soy sauce, dry sherry, cornstarch, and grated garlic. Add the beef and marinate it for 20 to 30 minutes. Heat the oil in the wok and stir-fry the scallions for 1 to 2 minutes. Push aside. Stir-fry the asparagus for 2 to 3 minutes. Push aside. Stir-fry the beef 3 to 4 minutes, until done. Return the vegetables to the beef. Stir in the hoisin sauce and peanuts and serve at once.

beef with snow pea pods and mushrooms

Yield: 4 servings

2 tablespoons vegetable oil
1 teaspoon grated fresh ginger root
1 clove garlic, grated
½ pound mushrooms, sliced into "T" shapes
14 to 16 snow pea pods, strings removed

1 pound flank steak, cut into thin slices
½ cup chicken broth or water
1 tablespoon cornstarch in 2 tablespoons water
3 tablespoons soy sauce
¼ cup cashews or peanuts

Heat oil in the wok and stir-fry the ginger, garlic, and mushrooms 1 to 2 minutes. Push aside. Stir-fry the pea pods 1 to 2 minutes or until they become bright green. Push aside. Stir-fry the beef 2 to 3 minutes. Return the vegetables to the meat. Add the broth, cornstarch mixture, and soy sauce and heat until sauce boils and is thickened and beef and vegetables are heated through. Add nuts and serve at once with rice.

beef with bean sprouts and mushrooms

Yield: 4 servings

2 tablespoons vegetable oil
¼ pound mushrooms, cut into "T" shapes
1 teaspoon grated fresh ginger root
1 pound beef (round, chuck, flank), finely sliced
2 tablespoons soy sauce
2 tablespoons dry sherry
½ cup chicken broth or water
1 tablespoon cornstarch in 2 tablespoons water
1 or 2 cups bean sprouts
2 stalks celery, cut into small cubes

Heat the oil in the wok and stir-fry mushrooms and grated ginger for 1 to 2 minutes. Push aside. Stir-fry the beef for 3 to 4 minutes. Return the mushrooms to the beef in the wok. Combine the soy sauce, sherry, broth, and cornstarch mixture. Stir and add to the beef and mushrooms. Heat until sauce thickens. Add the bean sprouts and continue heating just until they are heated through. Garnish with cubed celery and serve at once with rice.

Picture on previous page: beef with bean sprouts and mushrooms

beef with snow pea pods and cashews

Yield: 4 servings

1 pound beef (top of the round
    steak), sliced into ¼-inch
    strips
2 tablespoons black bean sauce
2 tablespoons soy sauce
1 clove garlic, grated
2 tablespoons vegetable oil
12 to 16 snow pea pods, strings
    removed
1 tablespoon cornstarch in ½ cup
    cold broth or water
½ cup cashews
1 cup bean sprouts (if desired)

Marinate the beef in a combined mixture of bean sauce, soy sauce, and grated garlic in a small bowl for 20 to 30 minutes. Heat oil in the wok and stir-fry the snow pea pods 1 to 2 minutes, until their green color brightens. Push aside. Stir-fry the beef 2 to 3 minutes. Return the snow pea pods to the beef in the wok and stir in the cornstarch and broth mixture. Heat until sauce boils and is clear. Add cashews and serve at once. (Bean sprouts may be added just before the cornstarch mixture is added, if desired.)

beef with celery and celery cabbage

Yield: 4 servings

1 pound beef (chuck or round), cut
    into 1-inch cubes
3 tablespoons soy sauce
1 tablespoon dry sherry
1 teaspoon sugar
2 tablespoons vegetable oil
1 cup celery cabbage (or bok choy),
    sliced diagonally across the
    stalks into ¼-inch slices

1 cup celery, sliced diagonally
    across the stalks into ¼-inch
    slices (leave may be left on)
¼ pound mushrooms, sliced into
    "T" shapes
1 tablespoon cornstarch in 2
    tablespoons water
1 cup chicken broth or water

Marinate the beef for 20 to 30 minutes in the combined soy sauce, sherry, and sugar. Heat oil in the wok and stir-fry the celery cabbage and celery for 1 to 2 minutes or until the light-green color intensifies. Push aside. Stir-fry the mushrooms for 1 to 2 minutes. Push aside. Stir-fry the beef 3 to 4 minutes. Return the vegetables to the beef in the wok. Add the cornstarch mixture and broth to the beef and vegetables. Heat and stir until sauce is thickened and clear. Serve at once with rice.

beef with oyster sauce

Yield: 4 servings

2 tablespoons soy sauce
1 tablespoon dry sherry
1 tablespoon cornstarch
1 teaspoon sugar
1 pound beef (chuck or round), cut
    into ¼-inch strips

2 tablespoons vegetable oil
1 green pepper, cut into ¼-inch
    strips
8 canned water chestnuts, sliced
2½ tablespoons bottled oyster
    sauce

Combine the soy sauce, dry sherry, cornstarch, and sugar in a small bowl. Add beef and marinate 20 to 30 minutes. Heat oil in the wok and stir-fry the green pepper strips and water chestnuts 1 to 2 minutes. Push aside and stir-fry the beef 2 to 3 minutes. Return the green pepper and water chestnuts to the beef in the wok. Gently stir in the oyster sauce. Heat through and serve at once garnished with nuts, if desired.

beef with bamboo shoots and peppers

Yield: 4 servings

1 pound beef (round or flank), cut
    into thin strips
2 tablespoons soy sauce
2 tablespoons dry sherry
1 tablespoon cornstarch
½ teaspoon sugar
1 clove of garlic, halved
2 tablespoons vegetable oil
1 green pepper, cut into ½-inch
    strips

1 red pepper (a green one that has
    vine-ripened), if available,
    cut into ½-inch slices
2 scallions, cut into ½-inch slices
1 8-ounce can bamboo shoots,
    sliced
½ cup chicken or beef broth

Marinate the beef strips in the combined soy sauce, sherry, cornstarch, and sugar for 20 to 30 minutes. Brown the garlic in the vegetable oil. Remove and discard the garlic. Stir-fry the pepper strips 2 to 3 minutes. Push up the sides. Stir-fry the scallions and bamboo shoots 1 to 2 minutes. Push up the sides. Stir-fry the beef 3 to 4 minutes. Return the vegetables to the beef in the wok and add the broth. Stir and heat until the sauce boils. Serve at once with rice.

Picture on next page:
(left to right on each
row starting at top)

a chinese feast featuring:
beef and pork with bean sprouts
curried pork with shrimp
beef with bamboo shoots and peppers
water chestnuts with bacon
chicken with peas and mushrooms
deep-fried pork with sweet-and-sour sauce

beef and pork with bean sprouts

Yield: 4 servings

½ pound finely chopped pork
    (butt or shoulder)
½ pound finely chopped beef
    (chuck or round)
2 tablespoons soy sauce
1 tablespoon vinegar
1 clove garlic, grated
1 teaspoon ginger root, grated
2 tablespoons vegetable oil
¼ to ½ cup green beans, cut into
    1-inch pieces
¼ pound mushrooms, sliced in
    "T" shapes
1 cup bean sprouts
½ tablespoon cornstarch in ½ cup
    chicken or beef broth

Marinate the pork and beef in the combined soy sauce, vinegar, grated garlic, and grated ginger root for 20 to 30 minutes. Heat the vegetable oil in the wok and stir-fry the green beans 2 to 3 minutes. Push up the sides. Stir-fry the mushrooms 2 to 3 minutes. Push up the sides. Additional vegetable oil may be needed. Stir-fry the bean sprouts 1 to 2 minutes. Push up the sides. Stir-fry the beef and pork 3 to 4 minutes, until well-done. Return the vegetables to the meat in the wok and add the cornstarch mixture. Heat until sauce is thickened and clear. Serve at once with rice.

beef shreds with carrots and green pepper

Yield: 4 servings

2 tablespoons vegetable oil
2 thin slices of ginger root
1 clove garlic, halved
1 large green pepper, cut into thin
    strips
2 carrots, shredded

1 onion, sliced
1½ cups bean sprouts
1 pound cooked beef, thinly sliced
2 tablespoons soy sauce
1 tablespoon cornstarch in ½ cup
    chicken broth or water

Heat oil in wok and brown the ginger slices and garlic clove. Remove and discard the ginger and garlic. Stir-fry the green pepper and carrots 2 to 3 minutes. Push aside. Stir-fry the onion 1 to 2 minutes. Push aside. Stir-fry the bean sprouts 1 minute. Push aside. Stir-fry the beef strips until heated. Return the vegetables to the beef in the wok. Stir the soy sauce into the cornstarch mixture and add to the wok. Heat until the sauce boils and thickens and the ingredients are heated through. Serve on a bed of boiled rice with shrimp crackers.

beef shreds with carrots and green pepper served with boiled rice and shrimp crackers

beef with chow mein noodles

Yield: 4 servings

**1 pound beef (top of the round),
    cut into ¼-inch strips
2 tablespoons soy sauce
1 tablespoon cornstarch
2 tablespoons vegetable oil
1 slice of ginger root
2 green peppers, cut into ¼-inch
    strips
1 onion, sliced
Chow mein noodles**

Combine the beef strips, soy sauce, and cornstarch. Allow for stand for 20 minutes. Heat oil in the wok and brown the slice of ginger. Remove and discard the ginger. Stir-fry the green peppers and onion 2 to 3 minutes. Push aside. Stir-fry the beef 3 to 4 minutes. Return vegetables to the beef in the wok and reheat. Serve at once garnished with chow mein noodles.

sweet-and-sour chinese meatballs

Yield: 4 servings

**1 pound extra-lean ground beef
¾ teaspoon salt
½ teaspoon pepper
½ teaspoon grated fresh ginger
    root
2 tablespoons vegetable oil
1 green pepper, cut into ¼-inch
    cubes
1 onion, chopped
1 carrot, grated
2 tablespoons vinegar
2 tablespoons brown sugar
1 teaspoon soy sauce
1 teaspoon dry sherry
1 tablespoon cornstarch stirred
    into ½ cup cold chicken or
    beef broth**

Blend together the ground beef, salt, pepper, and ginger. Shape into 1-inch meatballs. Heat oil in the wok and brown the meatballs on all sides for about 2 minutes. Add all remaining ingredients. Cook over moderate heat, stirring constantly, until mixture thickens. Cook an additional 5 minutes. Serve at once with rice.

beef stroganoff

Yield: 4 servings

2 tablespoons vegetable oil
1 medium onion, sliced
¼ pound mushrooms, sliced into
    "T" shapes
1 pound beef, cut into ¼-inch
    strips

1 tablespoon flour
¼ teaspoon salt
½ cup sour cream
½ tablespoon tomato paste
2 cups canned, fried potato sticks

Heat oil in wok and add the onion. Stir-fry slowly until transparent. Push aside and stir-fry the mushrooms 1 to 3 minutes. Push aside and add more oil to wok if necessary. Dredge meat in the combined flour and salt. Brown well in the oil. Return the mushrooms and onions to the beef in the wok. Add sour cream and tomato paste. Stir and heat just until heated through. Serve at once with potato sticks.

(clockwise from top) *beef stroganoff*
mushroom omelette
chicken and shrimp with vegetables

beef fuji

Yield: 4 servings

2 tablespoons vegetable oil

1 pound beef steak (round, chuck blade, or flank steak), 1 to 1½ inches thick, cut into thin strips

½ pound fresh mushrooms, sliced into "T" shapes

1 small onion, sliced

½ cup chicken or beef broth

¼ cup soy sauce

1 tablespoon cornstarch in 2 tablespoons cold water

1 8-ounce can bamboo shoots, sliced

1 8-ounce can water chestnuts, sliced

3 scallions, cut into 1-inch lengths

1 6-ounce package frozen, defrosted pea pods

1 1-pound can sliced peaches, drained

Heat oil in the wok and stir-fry beef, mushrooms, and onion for 4 to 5 minutes. Add broth, soy sauce, and cornstarch mixture. Cook, stirring constantly, until sauce thickens. Add vegetables and peaches. Continue heating until the vegetables are heated through. Serve at once with rice.

step by step to beef fuji
This recipe makes use of frozen pea pods and peaches which can be added to the heated sauce rather than be stir-fried earlier in the preparation.

Slice beef into thin strips. Partial freezing by placing the meat in the freezer for an hour may make this step easier. Prepare the vegetables according to the recipe.

Heat oil in the wok and stir-fry beef, onions, and mushrooms 4 to 5 minutes.

Add broth, soy sauce, and cornstarch mixture. Heat and stir until thickened. Add vegetables and peaches. Continue cooking until heated through. Serve at once.

completed beef fuji served with rice and miniature egg rolls

calves liver with bean sprouts

Yield: 4 servings

3 tablespoons dry sherry
1 teaspoon grated ginger root
1 pound calves liver, cubed into
    bite-size pieces
2 tablespoons vegetable oil
¼ cup blanched, whole almonds
2 medium onions, finely chopped
¼ pound mushrooms, cut into
    cubes

1 cup fresh or frozen, defrosted
    peas
½ cup chicken or beef broth
2 tablespoons soy sauce
1 cup bean sprouts
1 tablespoon cornstarch in 2
    tablespoons cold water

Combine the sherry and grated ginger in small bowl and add the cubed liver. Marinate for 20 to 30 minutes. Heat the oil in the wok and stir-fry the almonds for 2 to 3 minutes, until browned. Remove from pan. Stir-fry the onions with the mushrooms 2 to 3 minutes. More oil may be necessary. Push aside. Stir-fry the peas 1 to 3 minutes. Push aside. Stir-fry the liver 2 to 3 minutes. Return the vegetables and almonds to the wok. Add the broth, soy sauce, and bean sprouts. Stir in the cornstarch mixture and heat until sauce becomes thick and clear and bean sprouts are heated through. Serve at once with rice.

calves liver with bean sprouts

shredded beef with vegetables

Yield: 4 servings

1 pound beef (round or flank steak), sliced very thin and cut into strips 2 inches long

1 teaspoon sugar

1 tablespoon soy sauce

¼ teaspoon salt

2 tablespoons vegetable oil

1 carrot, cut into very fine 2-inch shreds

1 onion, sliced into ¼-inch slices

1 cup bean sprouts

1 tablespoon cornstarch in ½ cup chicken stock or water

1 tablespoon dry sherry

Marinate beef strips for 10 to 20 minutes in the combined sugar, soy sauce, and salt. Heat oil in wok and stir-fry the carrot shreds and onion rings 2 to 3 minutes. Push aside. Stir-fry the bean sprouts 1 to 2 minutes. Push aside. Stir-fry strips of beef 2 to 3 minutes. Return vegetables to the beef in the wok. Combine the cornstarch mixture and dry sherry. Add to the beef and vegetables and heat and stir until sauce is thickened. Serve at once with fried rice.

(right) shredded beef with vegetables
(left) fried rice with chicken and ham

chicken

sweet-and-sour chicken
with cucumbers and cantaloupe

Yield: 4 servings

4 chicken-breast halves, skinned, boned, and cut into bite-size cubes
1½ tablespoons soy sauce
1 tablespoon dry sherry
1 tablespoon cornstarch
2 tablespoons vegetable oil
1 cucumber, cut into bite-size cubes after the skin has been scored lengthwise with the tines of a fork (seeds may be removed)
¼ to ½ cantaloupe, seeded, rinded, and cut into bite-size pieces
1 sweet red pepper (if available), cubed
2 ounces blanched, whole almonds

sauce

3 tablespoons brown sugar
3 tablespoons vinegar
½ cup pineapple juice
1 teaspoon soy sauce
1 tablespoon cornstarch in 2 tablespoons cold water

Marinate the chicken cubes in the combined soy sauce, dry sherry, and cornstarch while remaining ingredients are being prepared. Heat the oil in the wok and stir-fry the chicken mixture for 3 to 4 minutes. Add the cucumber, cantaloupe, and red pepper (if used). Combine the ingredients for the sweet-and-sour sauce and add these to the wok. Stir gently and heat until the sauce boils and the cucumber and melon are heated through. Serve at once garnished with almonds.

31

sweet-and-sour chicken with cucumbers and cantaloupe

chicken with asparagus

Yield: 4 servings

2 tablespoons vegetable oil
1 clove garlic
1 pound asparagus, cut diagonally
    into ½-inch slices (discard
    tough, white portions)
4 chicken breasts, boned, skinned,
    and cut into ¾-inch cubes

1 tablespoon dry sherry
2 tablespoons black bean sauce
    (optional)
1 tablespoon cornstarch in ½ cup
    cold chicken broth
1 teaspoon salt

Heat oil in the wok and brown the garlic to flavor the oil. Remove and discard the garlic. Stir-fry asparagus 2 to 3 minutes. Push aside. Stir-fry chicken 3 to 4 minutes, until done. Return the asparagus. Combine the sherry, bean sauce, cornstarch mixture, and salt. Add to the chicken and asparagus and heat until sauce thickens. Serve at once with rice or noodles.

chicken with bean sprouts and snow pea pods

Yield: 4 servings

4 chicken-breast halves, skinned,
    boned, and cut into bite-size
    pieces
¼ cup white wine (or dry sherry)
½ teaspoon salt
2 tablespoons vegetable oil
2 cups fresh bean sprouts
1 cup snow pea pods, strings
    removed
½ teaspoon salt
½ cup chicken broth
1 tablespoon cornstarch in 2
    tablespoons water
Sesame seeds, toasted (optional)

Combine the chicken, wine, and ½ teaspoon salt. Let stand about 20 minutes. Heat oil in the wok and stir-fry bean sprouts 1 minute. Push aside. Stir-fry pea pods 1 to 2 minutes, until their green color intensifies. Push aside. Add the chicken and wine mixture and stir-fry 3 to 4 minutes, until the chicken is done. Return the bean sprouts and pea pods to the chicken in the wok. Add the combined ½ teaspoon salt, chicken broth, and the cornstarch mixture. Heat and stir gently until mixture thickens. Serve at once garnished with sesame seeds.

chicken with mushrooms (moo goo gai pan)

Yield: 4 servings

4 chicken-breast halves, boned, skinned, and cut into ½-inch cubes
¼ cup dry white wine
½ teaspoon salt
2 scallions, cut into ½-inch slices
½ cup celery, cut into ½-inch cubes
1 tablespoon vegetable oil
12 snow pea pods, strings removed

¼ pound mushrooms, sliced into "T" shapes
6 water chestnuts, sliced
½ cup chicken broth
1 tablespoon cornstarch in 2 tablespoons cold water
½ teaspoon salt
Whole, blanched almonds (optional)

Combine the chicken with the wine and ½ teaspoon salt. Set aside. Stir-fry the scallions and celery in oil for 1 minute. Push aside. Stir-fry the snow pea pods 2 minutes. Push aside. Stir-fry mushrooms and water chestnuts 1 to 2 minutes. Push aside. Add the chicken and wine and stir-fry 2 to 3 minutes, until chicken is done. Combine the chicken and vegetables in the wok. Stir together the broth, cornstarch mixture, and another ½ teaspoon salt. Add slowly to the chicken and vegetables in the wok and heat until thickened and clear. Serve over rice and sprinkle with almonds, if desired.

chicken with hoisin sauce

Yield: 4 servings

4 chicken-breast halves, boned, skinned, and cut into ¾-inch cubes
1 tablespoon cornstarch
1 tablespoon dry sherry
1 tablespoon soy sauce
1 green pepper, cut into ½-inch squares

1 tablespoon vegetable oil
½ pound mushrooms, cut into ½-inch cubes
2½ tablespoons hoisin sauce
¼ cup cashews

Sprinkle the cubed chicken with cornstarch, dry sherry, and soy sauce. Toss to coat well, and set aside. Stir-fry the green pepper in the oil for 1 minute. Push aside. Add mushrooms. Stir-fry for 1 to 2 minutes. Push aside. Stir-fry chicken 2 to 3 minutes, until done. Add hoisin sauce and cashews. Reheat, and stir briefly. Serve at once.

chicken with walnuts

Yield: 4 servings

4 chicken-breast halves, skinned,
    boned, and cut into ¾-inch
    cubes
3 tablespoons soy sauce
1 teaspoon sugar
2 tablespoons vegetable oil
1 cup English walnuts
1 teaspoon grated ginger root
1 clove garlic, grated
½ cup chicken broth or water
1 tablespoon cornstarch in 2
    tablespoons cold water
1 8-ounce can bamboo shoots,
    drained and sliced

Marinate chicken in soy sauce and sugar in a small bowl for 20 minutes. Heat oil in the wok and stir-fry walnuts 2 minutes. Remove from pan. Add chicken, ginger, garlic, and the marinade to the wok and stir-fry 3 to 4 minutes, until chicken is done. Combine the broth and cornstarch mixture. Add to the chicken along with the bamboo shoots. Heat and stir gently until sauce is thickened and bamboo shoots are hot. Add walnuts and serve at once with rice.

chicken wings with oyster sauce

This recipe is included among the stir-fried dishes because, although it is not prepared by stir-frying, it offers a delicious way to prepare chicken wings that may be left over from boning the chicken breasts called for in many chicken recipes given here.

Yield: 4 servings

2 pounds chicken wings (tips may
    be removed, if you wish)
3 slices fresh ginger root
1 clove garlic, crushed
3 tablespoons oyster sauce
2 tablespoons soy sauce

1 tablespoon brown sugar
2 teaspoons dry sherry
⅛ teaspoon 5-spice powder
    (optional)
1 cup chicken broth

Place the chicken wings in the wok and add remaining ingredients. Bring to a boil over moderate heat and simmer, covered, until the wings are tender, about 20 minutes. Remove lid and boil hard to evaporate all but about ½ cup of sauce. Eat hot, or chill and serve cold for a picnic lunch or as a snack. Yum! Can even be rewarmed.

chicken with green pepper and cashews

Yield: 4 servings

2 tablespoons vegetable oil
1 large green pepper, cut into
 ¼-inch strips
4 chicken-breast halves, skinned,
 boned, and cut into ½-inch
 strips
2 tablespoons soy sauce
1 tablespoon cornstarch
½ cup cold chicken broth
2 tablespoons dry white wine
½ cup cashews

Heat oil in the wok. Add the green pepper and stir-fry for 2 minutes. Push aside. Stir-fry the chicken 3 to 4 minutes, until done. Return the green pepper to the chicken in the wok. Combine and stir in the soy sauce, cornstarch, chicken broth, and wine. Heat and stir gently until the sauce is thickened and clear. Add the cashews and serve at once with rice.

chicken with celery and celery cabbage

Yield: 4 servings

1 tablespoon dry sherry
3 tablespoons soy sauce
1 teaspoon sugar
1 teaspoon grated ginger
1 broiler-fryer chicken, skinned,
 boned, and cut into bite-size
 pieces
2 tablespoons vegetable oil
1 cup celery cabbage, sliced across
 the head into ¼-inch slices

1 cup celery, sliced diagonally into
 ¼-inch slices (leaves may be
 left on)
¼ pound mushrooms, sliced in
 "T" shape
1 cup bean sprouts
2 tablespoons cornstarch
1 cup cold chicken broth
½ cup nuts (optional)

Combine sherry, soy sauce, sugar, and ginger in small bowl. Add chicken and marinate 20 to 30 minutes. Heat oil in the wok and stir-fry celery cabbage and celery 1 to 2 minutes or until green color intensifies. Push aside. Stir-fry mushrooms 1 to 2 minutes. Push aside. Stir-fry bean sprouts 1 to 2 minutes. Push aside. Add chicken and stir-fry 3 to 4 minutes, until done. Return vegetables to the chicken in the wok. Stir cornstarch into the broth and add to the combined mixture of chicken and vegetables. Heat until sauce is thickened and clear. Serve at once with rice. Garnish with nuts.

chicken with green peppers and bamboo shoots in oyster sauce

Yield: 4 servings

2 tablespoons vegetable oil
1 large green pepper, cut into
    ¾-inch cubes
¼ cup sliced bamboo shoots
¼ pound small whole mushrooms
    (or large ones, quartered)
4 chicken-breast halves, skinned,
    boned and cut into bite-size
    pieces

sauce

1 small onion, sliced (or 1 scallion,
    sliced)
2 tablespoons soy sauce
2 tablespoons oyster sauce
½ cup chicken broth
1 tablespoon brown sugar
1 teaspoon grated ginger root
1 tablespoon cornstarch in 2
    tablespoons cold water

Heat oil in wok and stir-fry green pepper 2 to 3 minutes. Push aside. Add bamboo shoots and mushrooms. Stir-fry 2 to 3 minutes. Push aside. Add chicken and stir-fry 3 to 4 minutes, until done. Return vegetables to the chicken in the wok.

Immediately add a sauce made by simmering together the sliced onion, soy sauce, oyster sauce, broth, sugar, ginger root, and cornstarch mixture for about 10 minutes. Heat this mixture with the chicken and vegetables for 2 to 3 minutes. Serve at once with rice.

chicken with green peppers and bamboo shoots in oyster sauce

chicken and shrimp with vegetables

Yield: 4 servings

2 chicken-breast halves, skinned, boned, and cut into ¼-inch strips
1 tablespoon dry sherry
2 tablespoons soy sauce
2 tablespoons oil
2 cups mixed vegetables (green beans, sliced mushrooms, strips of green pepper, shredded carrots, etc.)
½ cup chicken broth

1 tablespoon cornstarch in 2 tablespoons cold water
½ pound cooked whole shrimps
8 ounces thin spaghetti noodles, cooked according to package directions and tossed with 1 tablespoon soy sauce
1 egg, beaten and cooked in a small skillet over moderate heat as an omelette

Marinate chicken in sherry and soy sauce for about 20 minutes. Heat oil in wok and stir-fry vegetables for 2 to 3 minutes. Push aside. Add chicken, and stir-fry for 3 to 4 minutes, until done. Return the vegetables to the chicken in the wok. Add the broth, cornstarch mixture, and the cooked shrimps. Heat until sauce boils and shrimps are heated through. Serve over spaghetti noodles and garnish with the 1-egg omelette cut into ¼ inch strips.

shredded chicken with almonds

Yield: 4 servings

2 tablespoons vegetable oil
¼ cup whole, blanched almonds
1 medium onion, chopped
1 teaspoon ginger root, grated
4 chicken-breast halves, skinned, boned, and sliced into ½-inch strips
2 tablespoons soy sauce
1 tablespoon dry sherry
1 teaspoon sugar

Heat oil in the wok and stir-fry almonds 1 to 2 minutes, until golden. Remove from pan. Stir-fry onion and ginger 2 to 3 minutes. Add chicken and continue to stir-fry 3 to 4 minutes, until done. Return almonds to pan. Combine soy sauce, sherry, and sugar. Pour over chicken mixture. Heat and serve at once.

chicken with celery and mushrooms

Yield: 4 servings

2 tablespoons vegetable oil
3 to 4 stalks celery, cut into ¼-inch
    slices
¼ pound whole small mushrooms
1 broiler-fryer chicken, skinned,
    boned, and cut into ½-inch
    strips
½ cup chicken broth or water
1 tablespoon soy sauce
1 tablespoon cornstarch in 2
    tablespoons water
¼ cup dry sherry

Heat oil in wok and stir-fry celery and mushrooms 2 to 3 minutes. Push aside. Stir-fry chicken 3 to 4 minutes or until done. Combine chicken and vegetables. Add broth, soy sauce, cornstarch mixture, and sherry. Heat until sauce boils and is thickened, stirring constantly. Serve at once with rice.

pineapple chicken with sweet-and-sour sauce

Yield: 4 servings

2 tablespoons vegetable oil
1 green pepper, cut into ¼-inch
    strips
1 broiler-fryer chicken, skinned,
    boned, and cut into ½-inch
    cubes
1 8-ounce can pineapple rings,
    drained and cut into bite-size
    pieces

sauce

½ cup chicken broth
¼ cup reserved syrup from canned
    pineapple
¼ cup dry sherry or white wine
1 tablespoon vinegar
1 tablespoon cornstarch in 2
    tablespoons cold water
2 tablespoons orange marmalade
1 tablespoon soy sauce
1 teaspoon grated ginger root

Heat oil in wok and stir-fry green pepper 1 to 2 minutes. Push aside. Stir-fry chicken 3 to 4 minutes, until done. Return green peppers to the chicken; add pineapple. Combine sauce ingredients and add to the wok. Heat and stir until sauce is thickened and clear. Serve immediately with rice.

(clockwise from top)
shrimp with chicken and cauliflower
pineapple chicken with sweet-and-sour sauce
chicken with celery and mushrooms

40

chicken with sweet-and-sour tomato sauce

Yield: 4 servings

2 tablespoons vegetable oil
1 green pepper, cut into bite-size
squares
1 medium onion, cubed
1 carrot, very thinly sliced
4 chicken-breast halves, skinned,
boned, and cut into bite-size
pieces
1 cup pineapple chunks

sauce
2 tablespoons vinegar
3 tablespoons orange marmalade
1 8-ounce can tomato sauce

In a small saucepan heat the combined vinegar, orange marmalade, and tomato sauce. Heat oil in the wok and stir fry the green pepper, onion, and carrot slices for about 2 minutes. Push aside. Stir-fry the chicken 3 to 4 minutes, until done. Return the vegetables to the chicken. Add the sauce and the pineapple and heat through. Serve with rice.

chicken with peas and mushrooms

Yield: 4 servings

4 chicken-breast halves, skinned,
boned, and cut into ¼-inch
strips
2 tablespoons soy sauce
2 tablespoons dry sherry
½ teaspoon grated ginger root
1 tablespoon cornstarch
2 tablespoons vegetable oil
¼ pound mushrooms, sliced in
"T" shapes
1 cup peas, fresh or defrosted
frozen
¼ cup whole blanched almonds
½ cup chicken broth or water

Marinate the chicken strips in the combined soy sauce, dry sherry, grated ginger, and cornstarch for 20 to 30 minutes. Heat oil in the wok and stir-fry mushrooms for 1 to 2 minutes. Push aside, and stir-fry peas 1 to 3 minutes, until they are heated through. Push aside. Stir-fry the chicken 3 to 4 minutes. Combine chicken, mushrooms, and peas. Stir in the almonds and chicken broth. Heat until sauce boils. Serve with rice.

chicken livers with eggs and noodles

Yield: 4 servings

4 eggs
¼ teaspoon salt
1 tablespoon vegetable oil
**½ pound mushrooms, sliced in
    "T" shapes**
2 scallions, sliced

1 pound chicken livers, cubed
2 tablespoons dry sherry
5 tablespoons soy sauce
½ pound thin spaghetti noodles
2 tablespoons chopped parsley

Combine the eggs and salt and pour into an oiled skillet. Cook without stirring over moderate heat until eggs are set. Cut into ½-inch cubes. Heat oil in the wok. Stir-fry the mushrooms and scallions 1 to 2 minutes. Push aside. Stir-fry the chicken livers 1 to 2 minutes. Add dry sherry and 4 tablespoons soy sauce. Combine liver and vegetables and heat through. Add cubed eggs. Prepare spaghetti according to package directions; drain well and gently combine with 1 tablespoon soy sauce. Serve on a platter with the liver mixture. Garnish with chopped parsley.

*chicken livers
with eggs and noodles*

oriental chicken with chinese mushrooms

Yield: 4 servings

2 tablespoons soy sauce
1 tablespoon cornstarch
1 whole broiler-fryer chicken,
    boned, skinned, and cut into
    bite-size pieces
1 clove garlic, halved lengthwise
2 slices ginger root, ⅛ inch thick
2 tablespoons vegetable oil
½ pound fresh mushrooms,
    quartered through the stem
    and cap
4 or 5 dried black Chinese
    mushrooms, soaked 30
    minutes in warm water,
    drained, and diced
2 tablespoons black bean sauce or
    hoisin sauce

Combine soy sauce and cornstarch in small bowl. Add chicken, and marinate ½ hour. Brown the garlic and ginger slices in oil. Remove and discard garlic and ginger. Stir-fry fresh and black mushrooms 1 to 2 minutes. Push aside. Stir-fry chicken 3 to 4 minutes, until done. Add black bean sauce. Stir the mushrooms and chicken together and heat through. Serve over Oriental Vegetables.

oriental vegetables

1 tablespoon oil
¼ cup blanched almonds, slivered
2 green peppers sliced into ¼-inch
    strips (if possible, substitute a
    yellow pepper for 1 green
    pepper)
2 scallions, shredded in 2-inch
    lengths
1 8-ounce can bamboo shoots,
    sliced
Salt

Heat oil in wok. Stir-fry almonds 1 to 2 minutes, until brown. Remove from pan. Stir-fry green peppers, scallions, and bamboo shoots one at a time for 1 to 2 minutes each. Add salt to taste. Add almonds to the vegetables and serve at once.

Picture on next page: oriental chicken with mushrooms served over oriental vegetables

chicken with almonds and mushrooms

Yield: 4 servings

2 tablespoons vegetable oil

¼ cup whole blanched almonds

1 green pepper, cut into ½-inch cubes

1 medium onion, cut into ½-inch cubes

¼ pound mushrooms, sliced in "T" shapes

4 chicken-breast halves, skinned, boned, and cut into ½-inch cubes

4 to 5 water chestnuts, sliced

2 teaspoons soy sauce

2 teaspoons dry sherry (or white wine)

½ cup chicken broth or water

1 tablespoon cornstarch in 2 tablespoons cold water

Heat oil in wok and stir-fry almonds until lightly browned. Remove from pan. Stir-fry green pepper and onion 2 to 3 minutes. Push aside. Stir-fry mushrooms 1 to 2 minutes. Push aside. Stir-fry chicken 3 to 4 minutes, until done. Return the vegetables to the chicken. Add water chestnuts. In a small bowl combine soy sauce, sherry, chicken broth, and the cornstarch mixture. Stir and add to ingredients in the wok. Heat until sauce is thickened. Add almonds. Serve at once with noodles.

chicken with almonds and mushrooms served with noodles

barbequed spareribs

Barbequed spareribs have been included among the stir-fried dishes because they are often served with them. The spareribs can be prepared ahead and baked in the oven while the last-minute preparations are completed for the stir-fried dishes.

Yield: 4 servings

  **2 pounds pork spareribs,
     separated into 3 or 4 rib
     sections**
  **3 tablespoons honey or brown
     sugar**
  3 tablespoons vinegar
  2 tablespoons sugar
  3 tablespoons soy sauce
  1 clove garlic, crushed
  1 tablespoon dry sherry
  ½ cup chicken broth
  **⅛ teaspoon 5-spices powder
     (optional)**
  Spring onion flowers for garnish

Cut meat between bones with a sharp knife almost to the base so that pieces are lightly joined together. Blend together all remaining ingredients and pour over meat. Cover and refrigerate for 8 to 12 hours or overnight. Place meat on a rack in a shallow pan and baste well with marinade. Bake uncovered at 325°F for 1½ to 2 hours. Baste occasionally with the remaining marinade and turn once during the baking time. Serve hot garnished with spring onion flowers.

spring onion flowers

Wash several scallions and cut away the root ends. Discard outer leaves. Cut each scallion into 2-inch pieces. With a sharp knife cut a third of the way down into each end several times. Place scallions in a bowl of ice water for 4 hours or overnight, and cut sections will spread open to form "flowers."

pork with oyster sauce

Yield: 4 servings

1 pound lean pork, cut into 1-inch
    cubes
3 scallions, cut into ½-inch slices
½ cup chicken broth
2 tablespoons soy sauce
2 tablespoons oyster sauce
1 tablespoon sherry
½ teaspoon salt
1 tablespoon brown sugar
1 clove garlic, crushed
1 slice fresh ginger root

Combine all the ingredients in the wok. Cover and simmer for 15 minutes or until pork is done. Uncover and boil away excess liquid until only ½ cup remains. Remove the ginger slice. Serve with a stir-fried vegetable and boiled rice.

spicy chunking pork

Yield: 4 servings

1 slice ginger root
2 tablespoons vegetable oil
1 pound pork, boiled 1 hour and
    sliced very thin
1 8-ounce can bamboo shoots,
    sliced thin
10 to 12 water chestnuts, sliced
6 to 8 Chinese black mushrooms,
    soaked 30 minutes in water
    and sliced thin
3 tablespoons dry sherry
3 tablespoons hoisin sauce
1 cup sliced almonds or whole
    cashews

Brown the ginger slice in the hot oil. Remove and discard the slice. Add pork and stir-fry 2 minutes. Add bamboo shoots, water chestnuts, and mushrooms. Stir-fry 2 munutes. Add sherry and hoisin sauce. Stir and heat well. Add nuts. Serve at once with rice.

pork with peppers and cashews

Yield: 4 servings

1 pound pork, cut into ¾-inch cubes
1 tablespoon soy sauce
½ teaspoon sugar
2 tablespoons vegetable oil
1 small onion, cut into ¾-inch cubes
1 large green pepper, cut into ¾-inch cubes
1 large red (vine-ripened green) pepper, cut into ¾-inch cubes
1 tablespoon soy sauce
1 tablespoon cornstarch in ½ cup cold water or chicken broth
4 ounces cashews

Combine pork, soy sauce, and sugar and let sit while the vegetables are prepared. Heat oil in the wok and stir-fry the pork mixture for 4 to 5 minutes, until the pork is well-done. Push aside. Stir-fry the onion 1 to 2 minutes, add the green peppers, and continue to stir-fry for 2 to 3 minutes. Return the pork and add the combined soy sauce and cornstarch mixture. Heat and stir gently until the sauce is thickened and clear. Add the cashews and allow them to heat through. Serve at once with rice.

pork with peppers and cashews

pork and spring onions

Yield: 2 servings

2 tablespoons vegetable oil
½ pound pork (butt or shoulder),
    trimmed and cut into thin
    strips across the grain
½ cup chicken broth
2 tablespoons tomato paste
1 teaspoon sugar
1 teaspoon chili sauce
8 scallions, cut in quarters
    lengthwise, then into 4-inch
    lengths

Heat oil in wok and stir-fry pork strips 5 to 10 minutes, until crisp and golden. Combine remaining ingredients and add to pork. Simmer for 1 to 2 minutes. Serve at once.

curried pork with shrimp

Yield: 4 servings

½ pound pork (shoulder or butt),
    shredded into thin strips
2 tablespoons soy sauce
2 tablespoons vegetable oil
2 teaspoons curry powder
1 small onion, minced
3 celery stalks, cut into ¼-inch
    slices
2 scallions, cut into ⅛-inch slices
½ tablespoon cornstarch in ½ cup
    water or chicken broth
½ pound whole cooked shrimps

Marinate pork in soy sauce for 20 minutes. Heat oil in wok and brown curry powder and onion until the aroma becomes strong. Stir-fry the pork for about 4 minutes or until well-done. Push aside. Combine celery and scallions and stir-fry 1 to 2 minutes. Return pork and add cornstarch mixture. Heat until sauce is clear and thickened and shrimps are heated through. Serve with noodles.

sub gum ("many costly things")

Yield: 4 servings

2 tablespoons vegetable oil
½ pound pork, cut into thin strips
2 cloves garlic, crushed
2 chicken-breast halves, skinned, boned, and cut into thin slices
½ pound boiled ham, cut into thin slices
½ pound shrimps, shelled and deveined
1 small can bamboo shoots, sliced
4 or 5 water chestnuts, sliced
2 cups bean sprouts

sauce

5 tablespoons soy sauce
3 tablespoons dry sherry
2 tablespoons water
1½ tablespoons cornstarch
1 teaspoon sugar
¼ teaspoon pepper

Heat oil in the wok and stir-fry the pork for 6 minutes. Add garlic, chicken, and ham. Stir-fry 3 minutes. Add shrimps, bamboo shoots, and water chestnuts. Heat for 3 minutes. Combine the sauce ingredients and add to the wok. Heat until sauce is thickened. Add bean sprouts and continue heating 1 to 2 minutes, until they appear wilted. Serve at once.

sub gum ("many costly things")

mandarin combination

Yield: 4 servings

2 tablespoons oil

1 medium onion, chopped

2 cloves garlic, minced

1 green pepper, cut into ¼ x 1-inch strips

¼ pound cooked pork or chicken, shredded

2 cups cold, boiled rice

1½ tablespoons soy sauce

¼ pound whole shrimps, cooked

1 cucumber, sliced lengthwise, unpeeled

2-egg omelette, cut into ½-inch strips

Heat the oil in the wok and add onion, garlic, and green pepper. Stir-fry 1 to 2 minutes. Add cooked meat and stir-fry 1 to 2 minutes. Add rice, soy sauce, and shrimps. Continue to stir-fry until all ingredients are thoroughly heated. Cut the lengthwise cucumber slices crosswise every ¼-inch but not all the way through. They will hang together like a comb. Insert them here and there in the dish. Garnish with strips of egg omelette.

mandarin combination

szechwan

Szechwan dishes are characteristically hot and spicy. Stir-fried meats and vegetables are often coated with slightly sweet, thick, fragrant, hot sauces that bring out the flavor of many dishes. Szechwan cooking is considered by many to be the finest of the Chinese cuisines. Chili paste has been used in these recipes as the hot ingredient and has been reduced in amount for those who are not accustomed to peppery dishes. Ground Szechwan pepper, available in Oriental-food stores, or Tabasco sauce can substitute for the chili paste. Go easy on these, too!

szechwan duck

Yield: Approximately 6 servings

4- to 5-pound duck
2 tablespoons salt
1 tablespoon whole Szechwan peppercorns, crushed with a cleaver or with a pestle in a mortar
2 scallions, including the green tops, cut into 2-inch pieces
4 slices peeled fresh ginger root, about 1 inch in diameter and ¼ inch thick
2 tablespoons soy sauce
1 teaspoon 5-spice powder
3 cups peanut oil, or flavorless vegetable oil
¼ cup Roasted Salt and Pepper

Wash the duck thoroughly with cold water, and dry. Mix the salt, crushed peppercorns, scallions, and ginger. Rub the duck thoroughly with the mixture both inside and out. Place the scallions and ginger inside the duck and refrigerate overnight while covered with plastic wrap or aluminum foil.

Mix the soy sauce and 5-spice powder and rub it over the duck both inside and out.

Place the duck on its back on a platter inside a bamboo steamer, add water to the wok to within an inch of the steamer, and steam for 2 hours. Turn off the heat and let the duck rest in this position in the closed steamer for another 30 minutes. Turn the duck onto its breast, re-cover the steamer, and let it rest for another 30 minutes. Remove the scallion and ginger pieces and let the duck dry for 3 hours.

Pour 3 cups of oil into a wok and heat it to 375°F. Carefully lower the duck into the hot oil on its back and fry it for about 15 minutes. Move the duck periodically to prevent it from sticking to the bottom of the wok. Then turn the duck over on its breast and deep-fry as before for another 15 minutes.

When the duck is a deep golden brown on all sides, transfer it to a chopping board. Cut off the wings, legs, and thighs of the duck and chop them across the bone in 2-inch pieces. Cut away and discard the backbone and chop the breast, bone and all, into 2-inch squares. Serve the duck pieces, attractively arranged, with Roasted Salt and Pepper. Steamed bun dough pancakes make an excellent accompaniment.

roasted salt and pepper

5 tablespoons salt
1 tablespoon whole Szechwan
    peppercorns
½ teaspoon whole black
    peppercorns

Pour the salt and peppercorns into a hot wok. Turn the heat down to moderate and cook, stirring constantly, for 5 minutes or until the mixture browns lightly. Don't burn it! Crush the browned mixture to a fine powder. Strain it through a sieve and serve as a dip with Szechwan Duck.

szechwan beef

Yield: 4 servings

2 tablespoons vegetable oil
1 or 2 green peppers, cut into
    ⅛-inch strips
1 or 2 carrots, finely shredded into
    ⅛-inch matchstick-size strips
    (slice lengthwise, stack slices,
    slice lengthwise through
    stack)
1 scallion, quartered lengthwise,
    then into 3-inch-long strips
1 pound beef (round or chuck), cut
    into fine slivers or strips,
    ⅛-inch by 2 to 3 inches long
2 tablespoons dry sherry
2 tablespoons hoisin sauce
1 tablespoon black bean sauce
1 tablespoon vinegar
1 teaspoon sugar
¼ to ½ teaspoon chili paste (very
    hot!)

Heat oil in the wok and stir-fry the green peppers, carrots, and scallion for 1 to 2 minutes. Push aside. Stir-fry the slivers of beef for 1 to 2 minutes and recombine with the vegetables. Add the remaining ingredients. Stir and heat thoroughly. Serve at once with boiled rice.

twice-cooked szechwan pork

Yield: 4 servings

1 pound lean pork
2 tablespoons vegetable oil
1 large green pepper, cut into
    ¼-inch strips
1 scallion, sliced
1 teaspoon grated ginger root
1 clove garlic, grated
1 tablespoon black bean sauce
2 tablespoons water
2 tablespoons hoisin sauce
1 tablespoon dry sherry
¼ to ½ teaspoon chili paste (hot!)
1 teaspoon sugar
½ teaspoon salt

Cover pork with water and simmer, covered, for 1 hour, until done. Cool and slice into ¼-inch slices. Heat oil in wok and stir-fry green pepper for 1 minute. Add pork and scallion and continue to stir-fry for 1 minute. Combine remaining ingredients and add to pork-and-green pepper mixture. Heat thoroughly and serve at once with boiled or fried rice.

szechwan chicken (kang pao chicken)

Yield: 4 servings

4 chicken-breast halves, skinned,
    boned, and cubed into
    ¾-inch cubes
1 egg white
1 tablespoon cornstarch
2 tablespoons vegetable oil
1 cup unsalted peanuts or cashews
2 scallions, sliced
2 tablespoons dry sherry
2 tablespoons hoisin sauce
4 tablespoon black bean sauce
¼ to ½ teaspoon chili paste (very
    hot!)
1 tablespoon vinegar
1 teaspoon sugar

Combine the cubed chicken with the egg white and cornstarch. Refrigerate for ½ hour. Heat oil in the wok and stir-fry the chicken 3 to 4 minutes, until done. Add nuts, scallions, and remaining ingredients. Heat thoroughly and serve at once with rice.

56

shrimp and lobster

shrimp with lobster sauce

Lobster Sauce and Cantonese Sauce are made with garlic, fermented black beans, and egg. The sauce does not contain lobster, but is used with lobster, shrimps, and other seafoods. This is how the name was derived.

Yield: 4 servings

2 to 3 ounces minced pork
2 tablespoons vegetable oil
1 pound cooked shrimps, cut into
bite-size pieces
1 teaspoon grated ginger root
3 cloves garlic, grated
1 tablespoon black beans (dow
sei), washed and mashed
1 cup chicken broth or water
1 teaspoon soy sauce
1 teaspoon salt
1 teaspoon sugar
2 tablespoons dry sherry
1 tablespoon cornstarch in 2
tablespoons cold water
1 egg, beaten
Scallion slices, leaves only

Stir-fry the pork in the vegetable oil until well-done. Add shrimps, ginger, garlic, and beans. Stir-fry briefly. Combine broth, soy sauce, salt, sugar, sherry, and the cornstarch mixture. Stir and add to the wok. Heat until thickened. Remove from heat and pour egg in slowly while stirring with a fork. Serve on rice and garnish with green scallion slices. The sauce must not be hot enough to coagulate the egg as it is stirred in with a fork. The purpose of the egg is to color the sauce and thicken it slightly.

shrimp with chicken and cauliflower

Yield: 4 servings

2 tablespoons vegetable oil
1 cup cauliflower, cut into
    bite-size florets and parboiled
    (cover with boiling water and
    let stand 5 minutes)
1 cup fresh or frozen, defrosted
    peas
½ pound cooked chicken meat,
    cut into ½-inch cubes
¾ to 1 pound cooked whole
    shrimps
2 scallions, cut lengthwise into
    quarters

sauce

½ cup chicken broth
1 tablespoon soy sauce
2 tablespoons tomato paste (or
    chili sauce)
1 tablespoon cornstarch in 2
    tablespoons cold water
¼ cup dry white wine

Heat oil in wok and stir-fry cauliflower florets 1 to 2 minutes. Push aside. Stir-fry peas 1 to 3 minutes. Push aside. Stir-fry chicken, shrimps, and scallions 2 to 3 minutes, until heated. Combine sauce ingredients and add to the vegetables, chicken, and shrimps. Heat until sauce boils and is thickened. Serve at once with rice.

sweet-and-sour shrimp

Yield: 4 servings

2 tablespoons honey
1 tablespoon vinegar
1 clove garlic, crushed
2 tablespoons soy sauce
1 tablespoon tomato paste
Pinch chili powder
12 large shrimps, peeled and
    deveined
2 tablespoons vegetable oil

Combine the honey, vinegar, crushed garlic, soy sauce, tomato paste, and chili powder in a small bowl. Add the shrimps and marinate in the refrigerator for 30 minutes. Remove the shrimps from the marinade and stir-fry in the oil for 3 minutes (less if cooked shrimps are used). Add the marinade and heat for 2 minutes. Pour shrimps and sauce into a hot serving dish. Stir-fried vegetables may be added if you wish.

shrimp in garlic sauce

Yield: 4 servings

2 tablespoons vegetable oil
1 small onion, chopped
1 teaspoon grated ginger root
4 cloves garlic, sliced
5 or 6 Chinese dried black
    mushrooms, soaked 30
    minutes in warm water and
    sliced

1 cup peas, fresh or frozen
    defrosted
1 pound cooked shrimps
½ cup chicken broth or water
2 teaspoons soy sauce
1 teaspoon salt
1 tablespoon cornstarch in 2
    tablespoons water

Heat oil in wok and stir-fry onion, ginger, and garlic for 1 to 2 minutes. Add mushrooms and peas and stir-fry 1 to 3 minutes. Add shrimps and continue to stir-fry 1 to 2 minutes. Combine broth, soy sauce, salt, and the cornstarch mixture. Add to wok and heat until sauce boils and has thickened. Serve immediately with boiled rice.

shrimp in garlic sauce

shrimp with bean sprouts

Yield: 4 servings

1 green pepper (or a red, ripe one),
**   cut into ¼-inch strips**
1 cup bean sprouts
1 teaspoon grated ginger
2 tablespoons vegetable oil
6 ounces cooked shrimps
1 tablespoon dry sherry
2 teaspoons soy sauce
Salt

Combine green pepper, bean sprouts, and ginger. Heat oil in wok and stir-fry vegetables for about 2 minutes. Push aside. Add shrimps and stir-fry until heated. Combine shrimps and vegetables and add sherry and soy sauce. Salt to taste. Serve hot with Crispy Fried Noodles.

crispy fried noodles

Yield: 4 servings

12 ounces fine egg noodles
2 cups vegetable oil for frying

Cook noodles in boiling, salted water according to package directions. Drain, and rinse thoroughly in cold water. Dry on paper towels. Fry handfuls of noodles in oil at 375°F, turning frequently, for about 5 minutes. Drain on paper towels.

shrimp with cucumber

Yield: 4 servings

1 pound shrimps, shelled and
**   deveined**
2 tablespoons white wine
2 teaspoons salt
1 teaspoon sugar
2 teaspoons cornstarch

2 tablespoons vegetable oil
2 cucumbers, quartered
**   lengthwise, seeds removed,**
**   and cut into 1-inch pieces**
1 scallion, sliced

Combine the shrimps, wine, salt, sugar, and cornstarch. Let stand 30 minutes. Heat vegetable oil in wok and stir-fry the cucumbers 2 to 3 minutes. Push aside. Stir-fry shrimps for 2 to 3 minutes or until they turn pink. Return the cucumbers and heat briefly. Serve at once garnished with scallion slices.

shrimp with bean sprouts served with crispy fried noodles

shrimps with mushrooms and celery

Yield: 4 servings

1 pound shrimps, cleaned and
    peeled
1 teaspoon salt
3 tablespoons white wine
2 tablespoons vegetable oil
1 slice fresh ginger root
¼ pound mushrooms, sliced into
    "T" shapes

2 cups celery, sliced diagonally
    into ½-inch slices
1 scallion, sliced into ½-inch slices
1 tablespoon cornstarch in ½ cup
    cold chicken broth

Combine shrimps, salt, and white wine. Marinate in the refrigerator for 30 minutes. Heat oil in the wok and brown the slice of ginger to flavor the oil. Remove and discard the ginger. Stir-fry the mushrooms 1 to 2 minutes. Push aside. Stir-fry the celery and scallion 1 to 2 minutes, until the color brightens. Push aside. Stir-fry the shrimps and wine 2 minutes or until the shrimps turn pink. (Frozen, defrosted shrimps should only be heated through.) Return the vegetables to the shrimps in the wok. Add the cornstarch mixture and heat until the sauce boils. Serve at once with rice.

lobster cantonese

Yield: 4 servings

2 tablespoons vegetable oil
2 tablespoons black beans, rinsed
    and mashed
2 cloves garlic, grated
1 teaspoon grated ginger root
2 to 3 ounces minced or ground
    pork
1½ to 2 pounds live lobster,
    cleaned and chopped into
    1-inch pieces or 1 pound
    lobster tails, split
    lengthwise

1 cup chicken broth or water
1 teaspoon soy sauce
½ teaspoon sugar
1 tablespoon cornstarch in 2
    tablespoons cold water
Salt and pepper
1 egg, beaten
1 scallion, sliced

Heat the oil in the wok and brown the black beans, garlic, and ginger briefly. Add pork and stir-fry for 1 minute. Add lobster and stir-fry for 1 minute. Add the broth, soy sauce, sugar, and cornstarch mixture. Cover and heat for 5 minutes. Remove from heat, season with salt and pepper, and slowly pour in the egg while stirring with a fork. This sauce should not be so hot as to completely coagulate the egg and turn it white. The egg should give the sauce a yellowish color. Serve at once with rice. Garnish with scallion slices.

vegetables and rice

stir-fried green beans with variations

Yield: 4 servings

2 tablespoons vegetable oil
1 clove garlic
2 to 3 cups green beans, washed,
    stemmed, and cut into 1-inch
    pieces
½ cup chicken broth
½ teaspoon salt
½ teaspoon sugar
1 teaspoon cornstarch in 1
    tablespoon cold water

Heat the oil in the wok. Brown and discard the garlic. Stir-fry the green beans for 3 minutes. Add the chicken broth, salt, and sugar. Cover and steam over moderate heat for 3 to 4 minutes, until beans are tender but still bright green and crisp. Stir the cornstarch mixture and add it to the wok. Cook, stirring, until the sauce is thickened. Serve at once.

variations

green beans with black bean sauce

1 tablespoon black bean sauce
1 teaspoon dry sherry
1 teaspoon sugar

Combine ingredients and stir into the beans just before serving.

green beans with water chestnuts

Add 8 to 10 water chestnuts, sliced, to the beans just before the stock is added.

green beans with sweet-and-sour sauce

Add 2 teaspoons lemon juice and 1 teaspoon sugar to the beans just before serving.

stir-fry broccoli with shoyu ginger sauce

Yield: 4 servings

**1 head fresh broccoli or 1 package
    frozen, defrosted broccoli**
2 tablespoons vegetable oil

sauce

½ tablespoon cornstarch
½ tablespoon soy sauce
⅛ teaspoon powdered ginger
½ cup chicken broth
½ teaspoon salt

Prepare the fresh broccoli for stir-frying by breaking off the branches from the main stem and slicing the branch stems very thin. Cut each floret into several bite-size pieces. Heat the oil in the wok and add broccoli. Stir-fry for 1 minute, cover, and steam for 3 minutes. Broccoli should still be bright green in color, crisp, but heated through. Serve at once with the Shoyu Ginger sauce that has been prepared by combining the sauce ingredients and bringing them to a boil, stirring constantly. Sauce may be served separately or poured over the broccoli in the wok just before the broccoli is removed.

chinese mushrooms and bamboo shoots with hoisin sauce

Yield: 4 servings

2 tablespoons vegetable oil
**½ pound fresh mushrooms, cut
    into "T" shapes**
**4 ounces bamboo shoots, sliced (½
    small can)**
½ teaspoon salt
**1 teaspoon cornstarch in 1
    tablespoon cold water**
2 tablespoons hoisin sauce

Heat the oil in the wok. Stir-fry mushrooms for 2 to 3 minutes. Add bamboo shoots and stir-fry 1 minute longer. Combine the remaining ingredients and add to the vegetables. Heat and stir gently until the sauce thickens and the vegetables are coated. Serve at once.

64

stir-fried bean sprouts

Yield: 4 servings

1 tablespoon vegetable oil
2 cups bean sprouts
1 tablespoon soy sauce

Heat the oil in the wok and stir-fry sprouts for 1 to 2 minutes or until heated through but still crisp. Serve at once sprinkled with a little soy sauce.

stir-fried chinese celery cabbage

Yield: 4 servings

2 tablespoons vegetable oil
1 slice fresh ginger root
1 pound Chinese celery cabbage (bok choy), cut diagonally into ¼-inch slices

3 stalks celery, cut diagonally into ¼-inch slices
½ teaspoon salt
½ teaspoon sugar
3 tablespoons chicken broth
1 teaspoon sesame oil

Heat oil in the wok. Brown and discard the ginger slice. Stir-fry the bok choy and celery for 2 to 3 minutes. Add the salt, sugar, and chicken broth. Cover and heat for 1 minute. Serve at once sprinkled with a little sesame oil.

trimming chinese celery cabbage in preparation for cooking

sweet-and-sour vegetable medley

Yield: 4 servings

2 tablespoons vegetable oil
2 medium potatoes, peeled and
    sliced very thin
2 medium carrots, sliced
    diagonally very thin
4 scallions, sliced
1 cup green beans
½ cucumber, unpeeled, sliced
    into ⅛-inch slices

sauce

1 tablespoon cornstarch
1 tablespoon soy sauce
1 tablespoon vinegar
1 tablespoon tomato paste
1 tablespoon dry sherry
2 teaspoons sugar

Heat oil in the wok and stir-fry the potatoes 1 minute. Add carrots; stir-fry 1 minute. Add scallions and green beans and continue to stir-fry until vegetables are heated through. Stir together the ingredients for the sauce and add to the vegetables in the wok. Add the cucumber slices and gently stir the vegetables and sauce until the sauce thickens and the cucumbers are heated. Serve at once.

sweet-and-sour carrots

Yield: 4 servings

2 tablespoons vegetable oil
1 slice fresh ginger root
1 pound carrots, cleaned and
    roll-cut into 1-inch pieces
½ teaspoon salt
½ cup chicken broth
1 tablespoon vinegar
½ tablespoon brown sugar
2 teaspoons cornstarch in 2
    tablespoons cold water
½ cup canned pineapple chunks
    (optional)

Heat the oil in the wok. Brown and discard the ginger slice. Stir-fry the carrots for 1 minute. Add the salt and chicken broth. Cover and steam over moderate heat for 5 minutes. Stir in the vinegar, brown sugar, cornstarch mixture, and pineapple chunks (if desired). Heat until sauce thickens. Serve at once.

tossed spinach with peanuts

Yield: 4 servings

1 pound fresh spinach, washed
    and stemmed
¼-cup peanuts (or more)

1 tablespoon vegetable oil
1 tablespoon soy sauce
Salt and pepper

Steam the spinach in a small amount of boiling water for only 2 to 3 minutes. Drain at once, pat dry, and cut into fine strips. Crush half the peanuts with a rolling pin or mince with a cleaver. Heat oil in the wok and add the crushed peanuts, spinach, soy sauce, and salt and pepper to taste. Stir-fry for 1 to 2 minutes. Serve garnished with the remaining peanuts.

celery and mushrooms

Yield: 4 servings

2 tablespoons vegetable oil
½ pound mushrooms, cut into "T"
    shapes
1 small bunch celery, sliced
    diagonally into ½-inch slices
1 teaspoon sugar
2 teaspoons soy sauce

Heat oil in the wok and stir-fry the mushrooms 1 minute. Add celery, sugar, and soy sauce. Stir-fry 2 to 3 minutes or just until the celery becomes a brighter green. Serve at once.

five precious oriental vegetables

Yield: 4 servings

5 to 6 Chinese dried black
    mushrooms
1 small head of Chinese celery
    cabbage
1 or 2 bamboo shoots
4 or 5 water chestnuts

2 tablespoons vegetable oil
1 cup bean sprouts
3 tablespoons chicken broth
1 teaspoon salt
2 teaspoons soy sauce
1 teaspoon sugar

Soak the mushrooms in warm water for 20 to 30 minutes, drain, remove and discard the tough stems, and cut the caps into strips. Wash the cabbage well, drain, and cut diagonally into ½-inch slices. Cut the bamboo shoots and water chestnuts into slices. Heat oil in the wok. Stir-fry the cabbage 1 minute, then add mushrooms, bean sprouts, water chestnuts, and bamboo shoots. Stir-fry all together for 3 to 4 minutes. Add broth with the remaining ingredients. Mix well and heat through. Vegetables should be tender but still crisp. Serve at once.

shrimp and egg fried rice

Yield: 4 to 6 servings

1 slice bacon
2 scallions, sliced
1 clove garlic, minced
3 ounces shrimps, cut into small
pieces
2 cups cold, cooked rice
1 egg beaten with salt and pepper
1 to 2 tablespoons soy sauce

Fry bacon in wok until crisp. Remove and set aside. Add scallions and garlic to wok and stir-fry in the bacon fat for 1 to 2 minutes. Add shrimps and stir-fry until pink (if frozen or canned shrimps are used, add while stir-frying the rice). Add the rice and stir-fry 4 to 5 minutes, until rice is golden. Pour the beaten egg into a well in the rice. Stir and heat until all the egg is coagulated. Crumble the bacon and add to the rice with the soy sauce. Combine well.

fried rice with chicken and ham

Yield: 4 to 6 servings

3 tablespoons vegetable oil
4 ounces cooked chicken, finely
chopped
4 ounces cooked ham, finely
chopped
2 scallions, sliced
2 to 3 cups cold, boiled rice
(prepared a day ahead and
chilled)
1 tablespoon soy sauce
¼ teaspoon salt
1 to 2 eggs, beaten
2 tablespoons cooked peas
1-egg omelette (optional garnish)

Heat oil in wok and stir-fry the chicken and ham 1 to 2 minutes. Add scallions and rice and continue to stir-fry until rice is hot and golden in color. Add soy sauce and salt. Make a well in the rice and pour in the beaten eggs. Stir and heat until the eggs are coagulated. Add peas and heat for 1 minute longer. Garnish with a 1-egg omelette cut into ¼-inch strips.

Picture on next page: fried rice sub gum

mixed vegetables chinese style

Yield: 4 servings

2 tablespoons vegetable oil
1 green pepper, cut into ¼-inch strips
1 medium onion, cut into ¼-inch slices
3 stalks celery, cut diagonally into ¼-inch slices
½ pound bok choy or white cabbage, cut into ¼-inch slices
Toasted sesame seeds

Heat oil in the wok. Add all the vegetables and stir-fry for 4 to 5 minutes or until they are heated. Serve at once sprinkled with sesame seeds. (You may also steam the vegetables in a small amount of water in the covered wok for 4 to 5 minutes.)

fried rice sub gum

Yield: 6 to 8 servings

3 tablespoons vegetable oil
1 medium onion, chopped
1 green pepper, thinly sliced
4 ounces cooked ham, diced into ¼-inch pieces
4 ounces cooked chicken, diced into ¼-inch pieces
4 ounces cooked small shrimps, left whole
3 to 4 cups cold, cooked rice
1 to 2 tablespoons soy sauce
2-egg omelette (optional garnish)

Heat oil in the wok and stir-fry the onion until it is translucent. Push aside. Stir-fry the green pepper for 1 to 2 minutes. Return the onions to the wok. Add the meat, shrimps, and rice and stir-fry together for 4 to 5 minutes, until rice is golden. Sprinkle with soy sauce and garnish with ⅛-inch strips of omelette.

vegetable and ham rice cake

Yield: 4 servings

2 tablespoons vinegar
2 tablespoons sugar
½ teaspoon salt
3 cups cooked, cold rice
2 tablespoons vegetable oil
3 carrots, cut into matchstick-size
    shreds
2 ounces mushrooms, sliced
½ unpeeled cucumber, sliced
3 scallions, sliced
2 tablespoons soy sauce
2 teaspoons prepared horseradish
    sauce
2 tablespoons light cream
4 slices boiled ham, shredded

Combine vinegar, 1 tablespoon of the sugar, and salt together with the rice. Toss well. Heat oil in the wok. Add carrots and stir-fry 2 to 3 minutes. Add mushrooms, cucumber, and scallions and continue to stir-fry until all the vegetables are very tender. Stir in the remaining 1 tablespoon of sugar and the soy sauce. Set aside.

Grease an 8-inch spring-form pan (or use an 8-inch square baking pan lined with plastic wrap extending well over the sides so the mixture can eventually be lifted out). Pack half of the rice in the bottom. Cover with ¾ of the prepared vegetables, then the remaining rice. Combine the horseradish sauce and cream and spread over the rice. Cover with the remaining ¼ of the vegetables and the ham shreds. Place a piece of waxed paper over the top and weight it down. Chill for 30 minutes. Remove weight and paper, then carefully remove cake from pan. Use a wet knife to cut cake into slices and arrange on a platter. Serve cold with a little soy sauce.

fried rice with ham

Yield: 4 to 6 servings

3 tablespoons vegetable oil
1 medium onion, chopped
2 stalks celery, cut into ¼-inch
    slices
2 cups cold, boiled rice

3 ounces cooked ham, cut into
    small strips
2 eggs, beaten with salt and
    pepper

Heat oil in wok and stir-fry onion and celery 3 to 4 minutes, until they are translucent. Add the rice and ham and stir-fry together 4 to 5 minutes, until rice is golden. Pour eggs into a well in the rice. Heat and stir until all the egg is coagulated. Serve at once.

chapter 3
steaming

stacked bamboo steamers

the wok as a steamer

The wok makes an ideal steamer. Water is added and a round cake rack or a bamboo steamer is set inside to rest on the sloping sides 1 to 2 inches above the water level. Water must not be so close to the food that it boils up onto it through the rack. Bamboo steamers are interesting, but unless many foods are to be steamed at one time (and this can be done by stacking several bamboo steamers), a simple cake rack may be the more durable, less-expensive choice. A square cake rack may be used as a rack in an electric frypan if you do not own a wok. It is difficult to keep the water in the frypan from bubbling onto the food, however, unless the rack is set on custard cups and the frypan lid is high.

Some foods are placed directly on the cake rack or directly on the bottom of the bamboo steamer. A layer of cheesecloth may be placed on the racks first to prevent foods such as fish from adhering. Other foods are placed on a plate or in a bowl that is set on the rack.

Bamboo steamers are used with their own lids. The wok lid must be used if a cake rack is inserted.

steamed fish with scallions and ginger

Yield: 4 servings

2 tablespoons vinegar
2 cups water
2 teaspoons whole pickling spices
1 to 1½ pounds fish fillets
    (flounder, perch, etc.)

1 teaspoon salt
1 teaspoon grated fresh ginger root
3 tablespoons minced scallions

Combine vinegar, water, and pickling spices in the wok. Place fish on a metal rack 1 to 2 inches above the vinegar and water so the water will not boil up onto the fish but steam can circulate freely around it. Combine the salt, ginger, and scallions and spread evenly over the surface of the fillets. Place the lid on the wok and steam for 10 to 20 minutes or just until the fish will separate into flakes with a fork. Serve immediately. (The vinegar and spices in the cooking water eliminate the characteristic odor in the kitchen of cooked fish.)

steamed fish with black bean sauce

Yield: 4 servings

2 tablespoons black bean sauce
1 clove garlic, grated
1 teaspoon grated fresh ginger root
½ teaspoon sugar

1 teaspoon vegetable oil (for
    non-oily fish)
2 cups water
1 to 1½ pounds fish fillets
    (flounder, trout, etc.)
1 scallion, sliced

Combine the bean sauce, garlic, ginger, sugar, and oil. Place 2 cups water in the wok and arrange fish on a rack 1 to 2 inches above the water so the water will not boil up onto the fish but the steam can circulate freely around it. Spread the bean sauce mixture evenly over the surface of the fillets. Sprinkle with scallion slices. Cover wok and steam until fish separates into flakes with a fork. Serve immediately. (Rack may be covered with one layer of cheesecloth before fish are placed on it. This will prevent fish from adhering to the rack.) *steamed sea bass*

steamed sea bass

Yield: 4 servings

2 sea bass, about 1½ pounds each,
   cleaned but with heads and
   tails left on
1 teaspoon salt
4 mushrooms, chopped
1 tablespoon soy sauce
1 tablespoon dry sherry

1 tablespoon finely shredded,
   peeled fresh ginger root
1 scallion, including the green top,
   cut into 2-inch lengths
1 tablespoon vegetable oil
½ teaspoon sugar
2 whole shrimps

Wash the bass with cold water and dry with paper towels. With a sharp knife make diagonal cuts ¼ inch deep at ½ inch intervals on both sides of each fish. Sprinkle the fish, inside and out, with the salt.

Lay the fish on a heat-proof platter ½ inch smaller in diameter than the bamboo steamer. Pour the chopped mushrooms and seasonings over the fish, and arrange the pieces of ginger and scallion on top.

Pour enough boiling water into the lower part of the wok so that it comes within an inch of the bamboo steamer. Bring the water to a rolling boil and place the platter of fish into the steamer with the shrimps arranged as shown in the picture. Steam the fish for about 15 minutes, or until they are firm to the touch. Serve at once in their own steaming platter.

some ingredients for steamed sea bass

spareribs with black beans

Yield: 2 to 3 servings

**1 pound pork spareribs cut into
    2-inch-long pieces**
**4 tablespoons black beans (dow
    see), mashed or minced**
1 to 2 cloves garlic, grated
2 scallions, sliced fine
2 tablespoons vinegar
1 tablespoon sherry
1 tablespoon sesame oil
3 tablespoons sugar or honey
½ teaspoon cornstarch
1 teaspoon salt

Boil the spareribs for 4 to 5 minutes to remove the excess fat. Rinse and drain. Combine all the remaining ingredients in a bowl that will fit in a steamer (or in the wok on a rack above boiling water). Add spareribs to the bowl and coat well with the bean mixture. Place the bowl in a bamboo steamer (or on a rack set 1 to 2 inches above the water level) and steam for 30 to 45 minutes or until ribs are tender. Serve at once.

pearl balls

Yield: About 20 pearl balls

**1 cup glutinous rice (available in
    Oriental-food stores)**
1 teaspoon grated ginger
1 egg
1 tablespoon soy sauce
½ teaspoon salt
1 tablespoon cornstarch
1 pound ground beef

Cover the glutinous rice with water and set aside for 2 hours. Combine the remaining ingredients with the ground beef and shape it into balls the size of small walnuts. Drain the rice well. Roll each meatball in the rice firmly so the rice will adhere. Place on a dish lined with a paper towel. Set the dish on a rack inside the wok. Fill the wok with water to just below the rack. Cover and steam for 20 minutes. Serve hot as appetizers with hot mustard sauce and soy sauce. The glutinous rice swells, when steamed, to resemble small pearls. Serve these as hors d'oeuvres.

steamed celery cabbage

Yield: 4 servings

**1 small head celery cabbage, sliced
    diagonally into ¼-inch slices**
1 tablespoon soy sauce
1 teaspoon sugar

Place the cabbage in a bowl and season with the soy sauce and sugar. Set the bowl on a rack inside the wok. Add water to the wok to a level below the rack. Cover and steam 15 to 20 minutes. Serve at once.

Other vegetables are prepared in the same manner. Adjust the steaming time for other vegetables.

dumplings and buns

These are filled with a great variety of delicious mixtures and deep-fried, boiled, or steamed before being served as snacks. They can be made with leavened or unleavened dough.

Yield: About 48 dumplings or buns

unleavened dough

2 cups sifted all-purpose flour
¾ cup cold water

Mix the flour and water with your hands or a large spoon in a mixing bowl until the dough becomes stiff. Knead the dough until smooth and let stand for 30 minutes. Roll with a rolling pin into a smooth sheet about ⅛ inch thick. Stamp out circles about 3 inches in diameter with a cookie cutter. This is then ready to be wrapped around a filling.

leavened dough

¼ cup sugar
½ cup milk, room temperature
½ regular small cake of yeast
**1 tablespoon lard or hydrogenated
    shortening**
2 cups sifted all-purpose flour

Mix the sugar and milk with the yeast and let stand at room temperature for 20 minutes. Chop the lard into small pieces, add it to the flour, and add both to the milk mixture. Cover and allow to rise in a warm place. When the volume has nearly doubled, knead again and let stand for another 40 minutes. Then use to make dough circles much like was done with the unleavened dough.

folding a dumpling or bun

1) Dumplings for steaming: Place a spoonful of filling in the center of the dough circle. Gather the sides of the wrapper around the filling, letting them pleat naturally. Squeeze the center of the now-cylindrical dumpling to pack the filling tightly. Tap the dumpling lightly to flatten its bottom and make it stand upright.

2) Dumplings for frying or boiling: Place a spoonful of filling into the center of the dough circle. Fold the circle in half across the filling and pinch it together at the center. Make 3 or 4 pleats at each end to gather the dough around the filling. Pinch along the top of the dumpling to seal the edges tightly together.

3) Buns: Place a spoonful of filling into the center of the dough circle. Gather the edges of the dough up around the filling in loose, natural folds. Bring the folds up to the top of the ball and twist securely together. Set the bun aside with its twisted side up. You may roll the bun between the palms of your hands to turn it into a smooth ball.

   After you fill the dumplings or buns, and before boiling, steaming, or frying, they should be stored aside, covered, for 15 minutes.

a tray of steamed dumplings

cutting out dough for dumplings

filling and folding a dumpling

making the dumpling stand upright

cantonese steamed pork dumplings

Yield: About 48 dumplings

**2 stalks bok choy (or Chinese
celery cabbage)**
**1 pound boneless pork shoulder,
finely ground**
**1 tablespoon Chinese rice wine, or
pale dry sherry**

1 tablespoon soy sauce
2 teaspoons salt
1 teaspoon sugar
1 tablespoon cornstarch
**¼ cup finely chopped canned
bamboo shoots**

With a cleaver or heavy, sharp knife, trim the wilted leaves and root ends
from the bok choy. Wash the stalks under cold running water, drain, and chop
finely. Squeeze the chopped cabbage in a kitchen towel or double layer of
cheesecloth to extract as much of its moisture as possible.

Combine the pork, wine, soy sauce, salt, sugar, and cornstarch, and, with a
large spoon, mix them thoroughly together. Stir in the cabbage and bamboo shoots.
Place a spoonful of filling in the center of a dough circle and fold into a dumpling
suitable for steaming.

Pour enough water into the base of the wok to come within an inch of the
bamboo steamer and bring to a boil. Place the dumplings into as many steamer
racks as are needed to hold them and steam for 30 minutes. Add water as needed.
Serve the dumplings directly on the steamer plate set on a platter.

sweet-and-sour sauce

simple version

Yield: About ½ cup

1 tablespoon cornstarch
3 tablespoons water
2 tablespoons soy sauce

3 tablespoons sugar
2 tablespoons vinegar
1 tablespoon catsup

Mix cornstarch and water in a custard cup. Mix soy sauce, sugar, vinegar,
and catsup in a small saucepan and bring to a simmer. Add cornstarch mixture and
simmer until it thickens and clears, stirring constantly. If too thick, thin with water.

richer version

Yield: About 1½ cups

½ cup chutney
½ cup plum jam
¼ cup cold water
1 tablespoon sugar
1 tablespoon vinegar

Combine ingredients in a small saucepan; simmer 1 minute. Cool; store in refrigerator.

indian spiced ground beef dumplings

Yield: About 48 dumplings

1 large onion, chopped
2 tablespoons vegetable oil
1 pound lean ground beef
1 tablespoon curry powder
1 teaspoon paprika
½ teaspoon chili powder (or 1
   teaspoon red pepper flakes if
   you like hot foods)

¼ teaspoon black pepper
½ teaspoon garlic salt
2 fresh medium tomatoes, diced
Salt to taste
1 can of peas (8½ ounces)
1 egg, lightly beaten
2 to 3 cups of oil for frying
Mustard Sauce or Curry Powder

Sauté the onion in the oil in the wok until golden brown. Mix the beef, spices, tomatoes, salt, and peas thoroughly, using some of the liquid from the can. Add the sautéed onion, and mix. Place a spoonful of the mixture into the center of a dough circle and fold for frying. Seal with the beaten egg and set on oiled waxed paper until ready to cook. Heat the 2 to 3 cups of oil to 350°F. Deep-fry the dumplings for 2 or 3 minutes, until golden brown, drain, and serve hot with Mustard Sauce or Curry Powder.

mustard sauce

Yield: About ¼ cup

2 tablespoons mustard
4 tablespoons cold water
½ teaspoon vinegar

¼ teaspoon salt
¼ teaspoon brown sugar

In a small bowl combine mustard with half the water. Stir to a smooth paste. Stir in the vinegar, salt, brown sugar, and, finally, in a thin stream, the remaining water. Store in the refrigerator.

curry powder
simple version

Yield: 1¼ cups

½ cup ground coriander
¼ cup ground cumin
¼ cup ground turmeric
¼ cup ground ginger

Mix well and bottle tightly.

less-simple version

Yield: ½ cup

¼ cup coriander seed
2 tablespoons saffron threads
1 tablespoon cumin seed

1 tablespoon mustard seed
½ tablespoon crushed red pepper
1 tablespoon poppy seed

Grind together in a pepper mill, mix well, and bottle tightly.

vietnamese fried dumplings

Yield: About 48 dumplings

**12 dried Chinese mushrooms
(optional)**
2 eggs, slightly beaten
1 tablespoon vegetable oil
**1 tablespoon fish sauce or soy
sauce**
1 tablespoon lemon juice, strained
½ teaspoon salt
⅛ teaspoon black pepper
**Pinch of chili powder (or 1
teaspoon red pepper flakes if
you like hot foods)**
1 small onion, minced
1 cup ground, lean pork
**1 cup cooked vermicelli, minced,
or cooked rice**
1 clove garlic, peeled, minced
**2 cups raw shrimps, shelled,
deveined, minced**
1 cup bean sprouts, rinsed
3 cups oil (for deep-fat frying)
Shredded lettuce
Sweet-and-Sour Sauce

Soak the mushrooms in warm water for 20 minutes, drain, and mince. Place in a medium bowl and mix with ½ the egg, 1 tablespoon oil, fish (or soy) sauce, lemon juice, salt, pepper, chili powder (or red pepper), onion, pork, vermicelli (or rice), garlic, shrimps, and bean sprouts. Place a spoonful of this mixture into the center of a dough circle and fold into a dumpling suitable for frying. Seal with the rest of the beaten egg and set on oiled waxed paper until ready to cook. Add the 3 cups of oil to the wok and heat to 350°F. Deep-fry the dumplings for 2 or 3 minutes, until golden brown, drain, and serve hot with shredded lettuce and Sweet-and-Sour Sauce.

northern-style pork dumplings

Yield: About 48 dumplings

½ pound bok choy (or Chinese
    celery cabbage)
1 pound lean boneless pork, finely
    ground
1 teaspoon grated fresh ginger root
1 tablespoon Chinese rice wine, or
    pale dry sherry
1 tablespoon soy sauce
1 teaspoon salt
1 tablespoon sesame seed oil
2 tablespoons peanut or vegetable
    oil
1 cup chicken broth, fresh or
    canned
¼ cup soy sauce combined with 2
    tablespoons white vinegar (to
    be used as a dip or sauce)

With a cleaver or heavy, sharp knife, trim the wilted leaves and root ends from the bok choy, and separate the cabbage into stalks. Wash the stalks under cold running water, drain, and chop finely. Squeeze the chopped cabbage in a kitchen towel or double layer of cheesecloth to extract as much of its moisture as possible.

Combine the ground pork, chopped ginger root, wine, soy sauce, salt, and sesame seed oil, and then add the chopped cabbage. Mix with your hands or a large spoon until the ingredients are thoroughly blended. This mixture can then be used as a filling for dumplings, folded and sealed for boiling or frying.

To boil: Bring 2 quarts of water to boiling in your wok and drop in the dumplings. Stir to make sure the dumplings are not sticking together. Boil for 10 to 15 minutes, adding additional water as needed. Serve the dumplings hot with the soy sauce and vinegar dip.

To fry: Place 2 tablespoons of oil into the wok and swirl it about. Place the dumplings, pleated side up, into the wok and cook until the bottoms brown lightly (about 2 minutes at low heat). Add the chicken broth, cover tightly, and cook until it has been absorbed (about 10 minutes). Add the remaining 1 tablespoon of oil and fry each dumpling at least another 2 minutes. Serve the fried dumplings hot with the soy sauce and vinegar dip.

steamed date buns

Yield: About 48 buns

**½ cup lard or hydrogenated
     shortening
2 cups canned red-bean paste
1 pound pitted dates, finely
     chopped
Red food coloring (optional)**

Melt the lard in the wok at moderate heat, add the canned bean paste and chopped dates, and cook, stirring constantly, for 8 to 10 minutes. Transfer the contents of the wok pan to a bowl and cool thoroughly.

Place a spoonful of the mixture into the center of a dough circle and twist into a bun form. Roll in the hands until a smooth ball is formed. Steam the smooth buns in bamboo steamer trays above boiling water in the base of the wok for 10 minutes. Serve hot directly in the steamer tray placed on a pan.

deep-fried date buns

Yield: About 48 buns

**1 pound pitted dates
1 cup shelled walnuts
4 tablespoons frozen orange juice
     concentrate
4 tablespoons grated orange rind
2 to 3 cups oil for frying
Confectioner's sugar**

Cut dates into chunks about 1 inch square. Place in blender one-quarter at a time, with one-quarter of the walnuts. At high speed blend into finest particles. Turn into a large bowl, add orange juice and rind, and knead into a large ball. Place a spoonful into the center of a dough circle and twist into bun form. Roll in the hands until smooth.

Heat oil in the wok to 375°F. Fry the buns 6 to 8 at a time until just golden brown. Drain well, cool, and sprinkle lightly with confectioner's sugar before serving.

chapter 4
deep-frying

the wok as a deep-fryer

The versatile wok is ideal for deep-frying. Its sloping sides will enable you to decrease the volume of oil normally used in deep-frying vessels. Some woks are available with a semicircular rack that may be placed above the oil for draining foods. The oil returns to the wok rather than draining into paper toweling.

Oil used for deep-frying in the wok must be vegetable oil and its temperature regulated carefully. Vegetable oil will withstand the high temperatures of 375 to 400°F necessary to cook and delicately brown batter-coated foods. If the oil temperature is too low, cooking time is prolonged and the food will absorb much oil before it is done. Hydrogenated shortening smokes when it reaches 350°F and is not suitable for deep-frying. Vegetable oil will begin to decompose and smoke if it reaches a temperature of 450°F and will give the food a poor flavor. Therefore, an electric wok or an electric frypan is preferred to maintain the correct oil temperature automatically. Only small amounts of food should be deep-fried together at one time. Adding many food pieces at once will lower the oil temperature, prolong the cooking time, and result in less-crisp, greasy-tasting food.

tempura

Tempura is a Japanese word used to describe food that has been cut into bite-size pieces, coated with batter, deep-fried in oil, and served with one or more sauces.

Traditionally, Japanese tempura is served by placing the deep-fried food on individual mounds of rice and pouring over it a sauce composed of dashi, soy sauce, dry sherry, grated white radish, and grated fresh ginger. Dashi is a fish broth. Chicken broth may be used as a substitute.

In this country the dish is often prepared directly at the dinner table by the host and hostess and their guests. Each person is given small individual bowls of sauces for dipping and each dips his own food into the batter and frys it.

general directions

1. Select 5, 6, or more assorted vegetables and meats. Prepare them by washing, cutting into bite-size pieces, and drying well with paper toweling so the batter will adhere properly.

2. Arrange the selected foods on a tray in individual bowls or together on a large platter.

3. Select and prepare a batter for the coating of foods and place it in a large serving bowl. If you wish, a second batter choice may be prepared as well.

4. Prepare several sauces to be used for dipping and seasoning the batter-fried foods. Place these in individual dishes.

5. Heat 2 to 3 cups of oil in the wok to a temperature of 400°F.

6. Use a mesh skimmer, tongs, or chopsticks and dip food into the batter. Allow to drain briefly, then drop the food gently into the hot oil. When done on one side, turn and brown it on the other side. Total frying time is usually 2 to 4 minutes, depending on the thickness of the food. Thinly sliced vegetables should be cooked only 1 minute.

7. Remove from the oil, cool on a plate or paper toweling briefly, and dip into one of the dipping sauces before eating and enjoying.

foods suitable for tempura

*Fish fillets, cubed Scallops
*Frozen or raw shrimps cut into butterfly shapes

by cleaning, leaving the tail intact, cutting along the back and splitting almost to the inner edge. Open and press flat to resemble a butterfly.
Chicken livers
Lobster, shelled
Pork, cubed and precooked
Ham, cubed
Frankfurters, cut into ¼-inch diagonal slices
Meatballs, 1-inch size, cooked
*Mushrooms, small whole or cut into "T" shapes
Onions, sliced into ¼- or ½-inch rings
Broccoli florets
*Celery, cut into ½-inch diagonal slices
*Celery leaves, in bite-size bunches
*Fresh spinach, stemmed and cut into 1½- x 1½-inch sections
Cauliflower, cut into bite-size florets
Carrots, cut into thin diagonal slices
Parsley
Watercress
*Green peppers, cut into cubes
Bamboo shoots, sliced
Water chestnuts, sliced
Sweet potatoes, sliced very thin
Green beans, tips and strings removed
Snow pea pods, cut in half diagonally
*Some of our favorites.

tempura batters

Any batter used for tempura must be thick enough to adhere to the food. It will adhere if the food is dry and the batter sheets off a spoon for 1½ inches before forming into large drops. If the batter is too thick, too much will adhere to the food and the coating, when fried, will not be thin and crunchy. All batters containing flour should be permitted to stand for an hour or 2. During this time, the flour absorbs additional liquid and the rubbery gluten softens. Beer as an ingredient also aids in softening the gluten. Overnight refrigeration is also acceptable.

If time is short and the batter cannot be allowed to stand, avoid over-mixing it. Beating it beyond the smooth stage overdevelops the gluten in the flour and makes the batter rubbery and difficult to use as a coating.

Select any one of the following batters.

beer tempura batter

Yield: Approximately 2 cups

2 eggs
1⅓ cups sifted all-purpose flour
1 teaspoon salt
1 cup flat beer

Place the eggs, flour, and salt in a bowl and mix well. Gradually stir in the beer. Beat just until smooth. Let stand 1 hour or refrigerate overnight.

golden tempura batter

Yield: Approximately 2 cups

1 large egg
1 cup water
1¼ cups sifted all-purpose flour

Beat the egg and water together. Add the flour all at once and beat just until smooth. Let stand 1 hour or refrigerate overnight.

light, fluffy batter

Yield: Approximately 2 cups

1 cup sifted all-purpose flour
½ teaspoon baking powder
¼ teaspoon salt

1 tablespoon oil
2 eggs, separated
⅔ cup milk

Combine flour, baking powder, salt, oil, egg yolks, and milk in a bowl. Beat until smooth. Let rest 1 hour. Whip egg whites and fold them into the batter just before use.

thin and crunchy tempura batter

Yield: Approximately 2 cups

1½ cups cornstarch
¾ teaspoon salt
¾ cup cold water
1 large egg

Combine all ingredients in a small bowl and beat until smooth. This one is thin and crackly.

hot mustard sauce

Yield: ½ cup

**3 to 4 tablespoons vinegar
(approximately)
½ cup dry mustard**

Add sufficient vinegar to mix the mustard into a paste the consistency of mayonnaise. This sauce is very hot.

ginger-soy dipping sauce

Yield: ¾ cup

**¼ cup soy sauce
1 teaspoon sugar
1 teaspoon powdered ginger
½ cup dashi (fish broth) or
chicken bouillon**

Combine all the ingredients in a small saucepan. Warm and place in dipping bowls.

tempura sauce for seafood

Yield: ¾ cup

**½ cup dashi (fish broth) or
chicken broth
2 tablespoons soy sauce
2 teaspoons sugar
1 tablespoon horseradish sauce**

Combine all ingredients and serve warm in dipping bowls.

tempura sauce for chicken

Yield: 1 cup

½ cup chicken broth
4 tablespoons soy sauce
4 tablespoons sherry

Combine all ingredients and warm in a saucepan. Serve in dipping bowls.

lemon dipping sauce

Yield: 1½ cups

1 cup cold chicken broth
2 tablespoons cornstarch
3 tablespoons lemon juice
½ teaspoon grated ginger
2 tablespoons soy sauce
1 tablespoon honey or sugar
2 teaspoons grated lemon rind

Combine all the ingredients in a saucepan. Stir constantly and bring to a boil. Serve in dipping bowls garnished with a lemon slice.

plum sauce

Yield: 1½ cups

1 cup plum, peach, or apricot
    preserves
½ cup chopped chutney or Indian
    relish
1 tablespoon sugar
1 tablespoon vinegar

Combine the ingredients and refrigerate for 1 to 2 hours. Serve in dipping bowls.

other suggestions for sauces

Grated white radishes
Horseradish sauce
Soy sauce
Bottled sweet-and-sour sauce
Hoisin sauce
Lemon wedges

deep-fried dishes with sauces

The first four recipes in this section contain pork, beef, fish, or chicken, each deep-fried in a batter and served with a sauce. Change the dipping batters, alternate the sauces, and many new versions of each recipe can be prepared. For example, the lemon sauce is delicious with either the deep-fried chicken or the deep-fried fish. Stir-fried vegetables or pineapple chunks may be added to the meats just before the sweet-and-sour sauces are poured for many additional variations.

deep-fried fish with sweet-and-sour sauce

Yield: 4 to 6 servings

1½ to 2 pounds fish fillets
Salt

batter for frying

1½ cups biscuit mix
1 cup water
2 eggs
¾ teaspoon salt
2 cups oil for frying

sauce

1 cup water
½ cup cider vinegar
6 tablespoons catsup
2 cup brown sugar
2 teaspoons soy sauce
2 tablespoons cornstarch
1 tablespoon sesame seeds,
    toasted in the oven on a
    baking sheet until light
    brown

Cut the fish into 1-inch cubes or ½-inch strips. Salt lightly. Combine the ingredients for the batter and stir until smooth and free of lumps. Dip fish pieces into batter and deep-fry at 375°F until golden brown, turning once. Drain on paper towels and keep warm, uncovered. Combine the ingredients for the sauce in a small saucepan. Stir constantly over moderate heat until mixture thickens. Pour over fish. Sprinkle with sesame seeds. Serve at once while the batter coating is still crisp.

sweet-and-sour pork

Yield: 4 servings

1 pound pork (shoulder or butt)
    cut into small, bite-size pieces

batter

1 large egg
¾ cup water
1 cup sifted all-purpose flour
½ teaspoon salt
2 cups oil for frying

vegetables

1 large onion, cut into 8 wedges
    and separated into layers
1 carrot, sliced diagonally into
    ⅛-inch slices
2 green peppers, cut into 1-inch
    squares

sweet-and-sour sauce

2 tablespoons sugar
2 tablespoons soy sauce
2 tablespoons dry sherry
2 tablespoons vinegar
1 tablespoon cornstarch in 2
    tablespoons cold water
1 cup cubed canned pineapple,
    well-drained

sweet-and-sour pork

Prepare the batter for pork by combining egg with water Beat in flour and salt until batter is smooth. Allow to stand about 1 hour. (Flour particles will take up some of the water.) Heat oil in the wok to 400°F. Dip the pork into the batter a few pieces at a time and place into the deep fat. Cook for 5 minutes, until cooked through and golden brown. Drain on paper towels, leave uncovered, and keep warm.

Combine onion, carrot slices, and green peppers. Stir-fry in a small amount of oil for 2 to 3 minutes. Combine the ingredients for the sweet-and-sour sauce and stir until cornstarch is well-distributed. Add all at once to the vegetables. Add pineapple chunks and heat until sauce boils and is thickened. Pour over pork and serve at once while batter on pork is still crisp.

deep-fried pork with sweet-and-sour sauce

Yield: 4 servings

1 pound pork, cut into ¼-inch
  strips
2 tablespoons vegetable oil
3 tablespoons soy sauce

frying batter

1 egg
¾ cup milk
1 cup sifted all-purpose flour
2 teaspoons baking powder
½ teaspoon salt
2 cups oil for frying

sweet-and-sour sauce

½ cup brown sugar
½ cup vinegar
½ cup pineapple juice
½ cup water or chicken broth
1½ tablespoons soy sauce

Stir-fry pork in oil 3 to 4 minutes or until well-done. Allow to marinate in soy sauce for 20 to 30 minutes.

Combine ingredients for the frying batter and beat until smooth. Allow to stand for 1 hour. (Flour absorbs some of the liquid.)

Dip pork strips in batter and deep-fry in oil at 400°F a few strips at a time until light, golden brown. Remove pork with a slotted spoon and drain on paper towels. Keep warm.

In a small saucepan combine the ingredients for the sweet-and-sour sauce. Bring to a boil over moderate heat, stirring continuously. Arrange pork in a serving bowl and pour sauce over immediately before serving.

deep-fried chicken with lemon sauce

Yield: 4 servings

4 chicken-breast halves, skinned,
  boned, and cut into ½-inch
  strips

frying batter

1 large egg
¾ cup water
1 cup sifted all-purpose flour
2 cups vegetable oil for deep
  frying

lemon sauce

1 cup chicken broth
¼ cup dry white wine
1 tablespoon soy sauce
1 tablespoon honey
Grated rind of 1 lemon
3 tablespoons lemon juice
1 tablespoon cornstarch
Lemon slices for garnish

Combine the ingredients for the frying batter and allow to stand for 1 hour. Dip the chicken strips in the batter and deep-fry in oil at 400°F a few strips at a time until light golden in color and the chicken is done. Use a deep-fat thermometer and control the temperature of the oil carefully. Remove chicken from the oil with a slotted spoon and drain on paper towels.

Combine the ingredients for the lemon sauce in a small saucepan. Stir constantly and bring to a boil over moderate heat. Simmer 1 to 2 minutes. Arrange chicken in a serving bowl and cover with the sauce. Garnish with lemon slices. Serve at once while batter coating is still crisp.

deep-fried beef with scallions

Yield: 4 servings

1 pound beef (flank or round) cut into ¼- x 3-inch strips

frying batter

1 large egg
1 cup sifted all-purpose flour
¾ cup water
2 cups oil for frying

8 scallions, sliced into ½-inch slices
1 clove garlic, minced
1 teaspoon grated ginger root
2 tablespoons vegetable oil
½ teaspoon salt
¼ cup dry white wine
1 to 2 tablespoons soy sauce
2 tablespoons black bean sauce

Combine batter ingredients. Let stand for 1 hour. Dip beef strips, a few at a time, into the batter and deep fry in oil at 400°F. Drain on paper towels and keep warm.

Combine remaining ingredients and simmer, covered, for 20 minutes. Place scallion mixture on a serving platter and top with deep-fried beef. Serve with boiled rice.

deep-fried beef with scallions

deep-fried scallops with sweet-and-sour sauce

Yield: 4 servings

1 pound scallops (cubed fish fillets
   may be substituted)

batter

1 cup sifted all-purpose flour
¾ cup water
1 large egg
½ teaspoon salt
2 cups oil for frying

sweet-and-sour-sauce

4 pineapple rings, cut into small
   pieces
Reserved pineapple syrup and
   water to make 1 cup
1 tablespoon cornstarch in 2
   tablespoons cold water
2 tablespoons vinegar
¼ cup brown sugar
1 teaspoon soy sauce
1 small onion, sliced
Few strips each of carrots and
   green pepper
2 cups hot boiled rice

Combine the batter ingredients and beat just until smooth. Allow to stand for 1 hour. Dip scallops a few at a time into the batter and deep-fry in oil at 375°F just until golden brown and done, about 3 to 4 minutes. Drain on paper towels.

Combine the sauce ingredients in a saucepan. Stir constantly while bringing to a boil. Heat until thickened and the carrot and pepper strips are heated through.

Place scallops on a bed of boiled rice and cover with the sauce. Serve at once while the scallop batter coating is still crisp.

deep-fried scallops with sweet-and-sour sauce

sesame pork with sweet-and-sour vegetables

Yield: 4 servings

1 pound lean pork, cut into ¾-inch
    pieces
⅓ cup soy sauce
⅓ cup dry sherry
1 clove garlic, crushed

frying batter

1 egg
¼ cup flour
¼ cup cornstarch
½ cup water
2 cups oil for frying

sauce

1 cup chicken broth
½ cup reserved syrup from
    pineapple chunks
½ cup vinegar
½ cup brown sugar
2 teaspoons soy sauce
2 tablespoons cornstarch in ¼ cup
    water
1 8-ounce can water chestnuts,
    drained and sliced

1 15¼-ounce can pineapple
    chunks, drained
2 green peppers, cut into ½-inch
    cubes
2 cooked carrots, quartered
    lengthwise and cut into
    2-inch lengths
1 tablespoon toasted sesame seeds

Combine the pork, soy sauce, sherry, and garlic Marinate for 2 hours in the refrigerator. Drain. Combine the batter ingredients and beat just until smooth. Let stand for 1 hour. Dip pork a few pieces at a time into the batter. Drain. Deep-fry at 375°F until pork is done and the batter coating is a light, golden brown. Drain on paper toweling and keep warm. (If you wish, you may precook the pork.)

Combine the broth, reserved pineapple syrup, vinegar, brown sugar, and soy sauce. Heat until the sugar dissolves.. Add the cornstarch mixture and cook until the mixture thickens. Add the pork, water chestnuts, pineapple, peppers, and carrots. Heat until the ingredients are heated through. Serve on chow mein noodles immediately, before the crisp batter on the pork softens. Garnish with sesame seeds.

step by step to sesame pork with sweet-and-sour vegetables

Cut pork into ¾-inch cubes. Prepare vegetables according to recipe directions. Marinate pork with soy sauce, sherry, and garlic in the refrigerator for 2 hours. Drain.

Prepare the batter. Dip several pork cubes at a time into the batter. Drain. Deep-fry in the wok until golden brown. Drain on paper toweling.

Combine the sauce ingredients and heat until the sugar dissolves. Add the cornstarch and water mixture. Heat until thickened. Add pork and vegetables. Heat thoroughly. Serve at once garnished with toasted sesame seeds.

completed sesame pork with sweet-and-sour vegetables
served with chicken egg drop soup, and chow mein noodles

egg rolls

These are called Spring Rolls in China because they are served during the spring New Years days. Only in America are they called Egg Rolls.

Prepare either the Shrimp Roll or Pork Roll Filling. The Pork Rolls will have a rather moist but crisp filling because of the added cornstarch mixture. The Shrimp Rolls will have a less moist interior filling, with crispy vegetables.

Egg Roll wrappers (or skins) are difficult to make because they must be rolled out paper thin. Beginners may prefer to purchase the wrappers ready-made from an Oriental-food store. These should be kept refrigerated and used within 3 to 4 days.

Two recipes are given for the wrappers. The traditional method is the rolled-dough type. The skillet method is somewhat easier, but the dough is a little softer.

egg rolls—general directions

Purchase (or prepare) egg roll wrappers and prepare one of the fillings. Place some of each filling in the center of each wrapper. Brush the edges with beaten eggs. Fold one corner in just beyond the center. Fold the corners on either side in to the center, overlapping one another slightly. Then roll down the remaining corner to form a cylinder. Cover with a damp towel while preparing the remaining rolls.

Deep-fry the rolls 3 at a time in 2 inches of oil at 375°F until the skins are crisp and light golden. (Chinese restaurants only partially fry them, refrigerate them, and then complete the frying just before serving. This causes the filling to be moist and not overcooked.) Drain on paper towels and serve with Hot Mustard Sauce and Plum Sauce (recipes are given under the Tempura section in this book).

how to fold egg rolls

1. Fold one corner in beyond the center:

2. Fold both side-corners in:

3. Roll down the top corner and seal:

skillet egg roll wrappers

Yield: About 20

2 cups sifted all-purpose flour
2 tablespoons cornstarch
1 teaspoon salt
1 teaspoon sugar
1 egg, beaten
2 cups water

Combine the dry ingredients. Add the egg and gradually stir in the water until the batter is smooth. Oil a 6-inch skillet. Pour ¼ cup batter into the center of the pan and tilt it to spread the batter evenly over the bottom. Cook over low heat until the edges pull away from the sides. Turn over and cook the other side. Remove and cool before using.

egg roll wrappers

Yield: 16 squares

2 cups sifted all-purpose flour
¾ cup cold water
1 egg
½ teaspoon salt

Combine all the ingredients with a fork and stir until the flour is moistened. Knead the dough until smooth (about 5 minutes). Cover and set aside for 30 minutes. Roll out on a well-floured board into 116-inch-thick 6- or 7-inch squares.

shrimp egg roll filling

Yield: 6 or 8

2 tablespoons vegetable oil
12-ounces cooked shrimps, minced
2 cups Chinese celery cabbage, sliced across the head into very fine shreds
8 to 10 water chestnuts, shredded
2 stalks celery, minced

1 cup bean sprouts
1 teaspoon salt
1 tablespoon soy sauce
1 teaspoon sugar
6 to 8 egg roll wrappers (6 x 6 inches each)
1 egg, beaten (for sealing)
2 cups oil for deep-frying

Heat 2 tablespoons oil in the wok and stir-fry shrimps, cabbage, water chestnuts, and celery for 2 to 3 minutes, until the green vegetables become brighter. Add the bean sprouts. Stir in the salt, soy sauce, and sugar. Place mixture in egg roll wrappers and seal with beaten egg. Deep-fry a few at a time in oil at 375°F, until brown and crisp. Serve at once.

crispy fried vegetables

Yield: 4 to 6 servings

batter for frying

1 cup sifted all-purpose flour	2 carrots
1 egg	2 potatoes
½ cup milk	1 stick celery
Salt and pepper	8 small cauliflower florets
Cut the following vegetables into	1 sliced onion
matchstick size strips:	2 cups oil for frying

Prepare the batter by combining the flour, egg, milk, and a little salt and pepper in a small bowl. Mix or whisk until the batter is smooth and lump-free. Batter should be thin. If it seems very thick, add more milk.

Thoroughly mix the cut-up vegetables into the batter. Let stand for ½ hour. Using a slotted spoon, lift out spoonfuls of mixed vegetables and drop gently into deep fat at 375°F. (Use an electric wok or a thermometer to maintain proper temperature of the fat.) Deep-fry for 2 to 3 minutes, a few spoonfuls at a time. Lift out and drain on paper towels. Serve as a vegetable at any meal.

crispy fried vegetables

pork egg roll filling

Yield: 6 or 8

2 tablespoons vegetable oil
¼ pound pork, finely shredded
1 teaspoon grated ginger root
4 to 5 mushrooms, shredded
2 scallions, cut into ¼-inch slices
¼ cup bamboo shoots, shredded
1 stalk celery, minced
2 cups bean sprouts
1 tablespoon soy sauce

1 teaspoon vinegar
1 teaspoon sugar
½ teaspoon salt
2 teaspoons cornstarch in ¼ cup
    cold water
6 to 8 egg roll wrappers (6 x 6
    inches each)
1 egg, beaten (for sealing)
2 cups oil for deep-frying

Heat 2 tablespoons oil in wok and stir-fry pork and ginger until pork is done. Push aside. Stir-fry mushrooms, scallions, bamboo shoots, and celery for 2 to 3 minutes. Add the bean sprouts. Return the pork. Stir together the soy sauce, vinegar, sugar, salt, and cornstarch mixture. Add to the wok and heat and stir until the sauce is thickened. Place in egg roll wrappers and seal with beaten egg. Deep fry a few at a time in oil at 375°F until brown and crisp.

crispy pancake rolls with pork

Yield: 8 rolls

Pancake batter to make 8 thin, 5- to
    6-inch pancakes
2 slices bacon, cut in small pieces
2 ounces chopped pork
1 onion, chopped
2 tablespoons vegetable oil
¼ cup mushrooms, chopped
2 teaspoons cornstarch in 2
    tablespoons cold water
1 tablespoon soy sauce
1 egg, beaten (for sealing)
2 cups vegetable oil for deep-fat
    frying

Prepare 8 thin pancakes, cooked on one side only. Combine bacon, pork, and onion and stir-fry in 2 tablespoons vegetable oil for 6 to 8 minutes. Combine the mushrooms, cornstarch mixture, and soy sauce. Add to pork and stir-fry for 2 to 4 minutes. Cool and place a spoonful on each pancake. Roll up and tuck ends in. Seal edges with beaten egg.

Heat oil to 400°F and deep-fry pancake rolls 2 to 3 minutes or until crisp and golden brown. Fry only 2 or 3 at a time or the temperature of the fat cannot be maintained. Drain on paper towels. Rolls are best served hot.

deep-fried beef cubes

Yield: Approximately 4 servings

Cooking oil
Slice of raw potato
2 pounds beef tenderloin or
      sirloin, cut in ¾-inch cubes
Meat tenderizer
Currant-Chutney Sauce
Deviled Roquefort Butter
Fluffy Horseradish Sauce
Sauce Diable
Curry Sauce
Chopped onions

Pour oil into an electric wok to ⅔ full. Use part olive or part peanut oil for flavor. Set to 425°F. Place a slice of raw potato in bottom of the pot to prevent oil from sputtering.

Have beef at room temperature and trim well of all fat. If you use sirloin, sprinkle with meat tenderizer, following label instructions.

Arrange the meat in the center of dinner plates with the sauces arranged in individual bowls so each guest can help himself. Provide guests with chopsticks or long-handled forks. Each guest picks up a piece of beef with chopsticks or fork and cooks it in the oil until the desired degree of doneness is reached. Dip the meat into one or more sauces, or into the chopped onions.

currant-chutney sauce

Yield: About 1 cup

¾ cup red currant jelly
⅓ cup chopped chutney
Juice of ½ lemon
Pinch of salt

Combine all ingredients in a saucepan and heat, stirring occasionally. Serve warm.

deviled roquefort butter

Yield: 1 cup

¼ pound soft Roquefort cheese
½ cup soft butter or margarine
1 tablespoon prepared mustard
1 small clove garlic, crushed
3 drops Angostura bitters

Combine all ingredients and whip until light and fluffy. Cover and refrigerate several hours to blend flavors. Let stand at room temperature to soften. Whip with a fork to fluff before serving.

fluffy horseradish sauce

Yield: About 1½ cups

1 cup sour cream
¼ cup prepared horseradish,
    drained
1 tablespoon lemon juice
1 tablespoon sugar
1 tablespoon minced chives

Mix together all ingredients in a bowl. Cover and refrigerate several hours to blend flavors. Stir before serving.

sauce diable

Yield: About 2 cups

1 onion, chopped
1 clove garlic, crushed
¼ cup butter or margarine
½ cup red wine
1 10-ounce can beef gravy with
    mushrooms
1 tablespoon Worcestershire sauce
1 tablespoon lemon juice
1½ teaspoons dry mustard
1 teaspoon salt
1 teaspoon pepper

Sauté onion and garlic in butter or margarine until golden. Add remaining ingredients. Simmer for 15 minutes, stirring occasionally. This may be prepared ahead and reheated just before serving.

curry sauce

Yield: About 1½ cups

1 onion, chopped
1 tablespoon butter or margarine
1 tablespoon flour
2 to 3 teaspoons curry powder
1 tomato, peeled and chopped
¼ cup chopped apple
1 tablespoon brown sugar
1 cup chicken broth

Sauté onion in butter or margarine until golden. Add flour and curry powder and stir until smooth and blended. Add tomato, apple, brown sugar, and chicken broth and stir until smooth and thickened, about 15 minutes. Flavor is improved by making this ahead and reheating just before serving.

other

If you are deep-frying other foods, try some Paper-Wrapped Chicken. The cooking parchment is available in gourmet-food stores and in many Oriental-food stores. Foil or bond paper may be used as a less interesting but more available substitute for the parchment paper.

paper-wrapped chicken

Yield: 4 servings

1 pound chicken meat, very thinly
    sliced
2 tablespoons soy sauce
1 tablespoon dry sherry (or dry
    white wine)
½ teaspoon brown sugar or honey
½ teaspoon salt
1 scallion, very thinly sliced
1 teaspoon grated fresh ginger root
16 pieces cellophane (cooking
    parchment) paper, 4 inches
    square (approximately)
2 cups vegetable oil for frying

Combine the chicken, soy sauce, sherry, brown sugar, salt, scallion, and ginger and marinate 20 to 30 minutes. Divide the chicken mixture into 16 portions and wrap each portion in a piece of cooking parchment and fasten well. Heat the oil in the wok to 375°F and deep-fry the packages a few at a time for 2 to 3 minutes. Drain on paper toweling and keep hot. Do not reheat. Serve wrapped to hold in the tasty juices. The diner unwraps each just before eating. Very flavorful!

how to wrap
paper-wrapped chicken

1. Fold the paper
   around the chicken
   in the order shown:

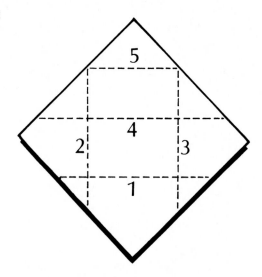

2. Tuck in the point
   of no. 5 securely:

chapter 5
hot-pot cookery

This allows you to stage your dinner right at the table and make the cooking part of the entertainment. These dishes can be prepared in a Mongolian cooker or an electric wok. Preparation by the guest is possible, much as in fondue or tempura cookery. A number of condiments and dips are normally part of the hot-pot scene.

Dips that may be used as purchased are:
oyster sauce
plum sauce
hoisin sauce
horseradish sauce
teriyaki sauce
chili sauce

hot mustard dip

Yield: 2 to 4 tablespoons

2 to 4 tablespoons dry mustard
Sufficient vinegar to make a paste

Combine the dry mustard with vinegar. This makes a very hot dip. Only a small amount should be used on foods.

soy-sesame oil dip

Yield: ¾ cup

½ cup soy sauce
¼ cup sesame seed oil
1 teaspoon sugar
2 tablespoons dry sherry

Mix all the ingredients together. Serve in dipping bowls. Recipe may be halved as sauce is thin and small amounts adhere to the food.

sweet-and-sour dip

Yield: Approximately 2½ cups

2 tablespoons cornstarch
¾ cup pineapple juice
½ cup brown sugar
½ cup vinegar
1 tablespoon catsup
1 teaspoon salt
cup crushed pineapple

Combine cornstarch and pineapple juice in a saucepan. Add the remaining ingredients and stir over medium heat until the sauce boils and is thickened.

pungent sweet-and-sour sauce

Yield: About 1 cup

1 cup bottled sweet-and-sour
**   sauce**
2 tablespoons catsup
2 teaspoons prepared mustard

Mix ingredients together and heat gently. Serve warm.

mustard cream sauce

Yield: About ¾ cup

¼ cup prepared mustard
1 tablespoon minced chives
1 teaspoon lemon juice
¼ cup sour cream
¼ cup mayonnaise

Blend together all ingredients and let stand several hours before using.

ginger-soy sauce

Yield: About 1½ cups

½ cup soy sauce
1 cup water
2 tablespoons white wine
**   (optional)**
2 teaspoons sugar
1 teaspoon powdered ginger

Mix together all ingredients and heat gently. Serve warm.

oriental firepot

Yield: Approximately 4 servings

1 pound sirloin or flank steak, sliced paper thin across the grain (slice flank steak on the diagonal)

2 chicken breasts, skinned, boned, and sliced very thin across the grain

½ pound thinly sliced red snapper fillet, or sole or haddock

½ pound sliced chicken livers

½ pound small spinach leaves, washed and trimmed of stems

¾ pound mushrooms, wiped and quartered

2 cups cubed bean curd or peeled and cubed eggplant

1 package (10-ounce) frozen snow pea pods, or frozen Italian-style beans, thawed

2 cups cherry tomatoes

1 bunch scallions, trimmed and cut into 2-inch lengths

Chicken broth or stock

¼ teaspoon ginger

Pungent Sweet-and-Sour Sauce

Ginger-Soy Sauce

Mustard Cream Sauce

Hot cooked rice

Prepare the foods as indicated in the ingredient list. This may be done several hours before serving time. The sauces should be prepared well in advance so that the flavors blend well. Keep food and sauces covered and refrigerated.

Shortly before serving time arrange meat, chicken, fish, chicken livers, and vegetables in small dishes or on plates. Set out the sauces and provide the guests with chopsticks or long-handled forks.

If using the Mongolian cooker, place 6 to 8 charcoal briquettes in the bottom section of the cooker, add charcoal starter, and light. On the range, heat enough chicken broth with the ginger added to fill the Mongolian cooker ⅔ full. Pour into cooker when hot. Cover and continue to heat until broth is just bubbling. Or, fill the electric wok ⅔ full with chicken broth. Add ginger. Cover and bring to boiling point. Adjust heat until broth is just bubbling.

Each guest spoons some of each sauce onto his plate, then picks up desired foods with chopsticks or fork, and lowers them into broth to cook. When food is cooked, he lifts them out with a wire ladle and dips each piece into one of the sauces. Do not try to cook too much food in the broth at one time, as the broth must always be bubbling slightly. Serve with fluffy hot rice. Add noodles to the remaining broth and when they are done ladle the soup into soup bowls for each guest.

chapter 6
red-stewing

A cooking technique native to the Fukien area of China is stewing in soy sauce. This is called "red-stewing" because of the red color imparted in the stewing process.

red-stewed shin of beef

Yield: Approximately 4 servings

2 tablespoons cooking oil
2 pounds shin of beef
⅛ teaspoon pepper
2 slices of fresh ginger root
1 garlic clove
1 scallion, halved
1 teaspoon salt
2 teaspoons sugar
¼ cup soy sauce
1 teaspoon sesame seed oil
1 teaspoon sherry
Water to cover the meat

Heat the oil in a wok; when it is hot, add the meat and brown on both sides. Add the pepper, ginger root, garlic, and scallion. Add the salt and sugar and pour the soy sauce, sesame seed oil, and sherry over it. Add enough boiling water to cover meat. Bring liquid to a boil, cover, and turn down heat. Simmer slowly for 2½ hours. Remove meat and cut into slices ¼ inch thick; arrange on a shallow dish. Pour gravy over it and serve at once.

red-stewed beef tongue

Yield: Approximately 4 servings

1 beef tongue
Boiling water to cover meat
½ clove garlic
1 tablespoon oil
2 tablespoons cooking wine

2 tablespoons dark soy sauce per
  pound of meat
1 teaspoon sugar per pound of
  meat

Immerse the tongue completely in boiling water, turn off the heat, and let soak for 1 minute. Remove the tongue from the water and use a blunt knife to peel off the skin.

Brown the garlic in oil in a wok, then brown the tongue on both sides. Lower the heat and add the cooking wine. For each pound of tongue, add 2 tablespoons dark soy sauce. Cook over low heat for 1½ to 2 hours. Turn the tongue at 20-minute intervals. Add water to maintain the quantity of cooking liquid at 6 to 8 tablespoons. During the last 20 minutes, add 1 teaspoon of sugar per pound and serve.

red-stewed beef

Yield: About 4 servings

1½ pounds beef
Water to cover meat
1 tablespoon oil
1 clove garlic

4½ tablespoons soy sauce
1 tablespoon sugar
1 tablespoon wine
2 slices ginger the size of a penny

Cut the beef into cubes 1 x 1 inch and simmer in a wok with enough water to barely cover for 15 minutes. Drain beef and brown it at medium temperature, using 1 tablespoon oil and 1 clove of garlic. Add soy sauce, sugar, wine, and ginger. Add the drained juice; simmer at low heat until tender. Complements that may be added during the stewing process are potatoes, turnips, Brussels sprouts, or carrots.

red-stewed pork shoulder

Yield: Approximately 6 servings

6-pound pork shoulder
2 cups water
¼ cup sherry
1 cup soy sauce

4 slices preserved ginger root
4 scallions
1 tablespoon sugar
Hot cooked rice

Wash pork well and pull off any hairs that may be on the skin. Place the meat, skin side up, in a wok with the water. Turn heat high; when water boils, pour the sherry, then the soy sauce, over the pork. Place ginger root and scallions in the liquid. Cover pork, lower heat, and simmer for 1 hour. Turn the meat and simmer for another hour. Turn the meat again, add sugar, and cook for 30 minutes longer. The meat should now be tender enough to give way with chopsticks. Serve on a bed of rice in a deep bowl, with the gravy poured over it.

soy sauce chicken

Yield: 4 to 6 servings

1 4½- to 5-pound roasting chicken
2 cups cold water
2 cups soy sauce
¼ cup Chinese rice wine, or pale dry sherry
5 slices peeled, fresh ginger root about 1 inch in diameter and ⅛ inch thick

1 whole star anise, or 8 sections star anise
¼ cup rock candy in small pieces, or 2 tablespoons granulated sugar
1 teaspoon sesame seed oil

Wash chicken and dry with paper towels. In a wok large enough to hold the chicken snugly, bring the water, soy sauce, wine, ginger, and star anise to a boil, then add the chicken. The liquid should reach halfway up the chicken. Bring to boil, reduce heat to moderate, and cook covered for 20 minutes. Turn the chicken over. Stir the rock candy or sugar into the sauce and baste the chicken thoroughly. Simmer 20 minutes longer, basting frequently. Turn off heat, cover the wok, and let the chicken cook for 2 to 3 hours.

Transfer chicken to chopping board and brush it with sesame seed oil. Remove the wings and legs and split the chicken in half lengthwise by cutting through its breastbone and backbone. Lay the halves skin side up on the board and chop them crosswise, bones and all, into 1 x 3-inch pieces, reconstructing the pieces in approximately their original shape in the center of a platter as you proceed. Chop the wings and legs similarly and place them around the breasts. Moisten the chicken with ¼ cup of the sauce in which it cooked and serve at room temperature.

stewed chicken with pork

Yield: 3 to 4 servings

1 clove garlic
1 small slice of fresh ginger root
8 ounces pork, cut into 1-inch cubes
8 ounces chicken, cut into 1- inch cubes
2 tablespoons cooking oil
4 tablespoons soy sauce

3 teaspoons sugar
3 tablespoons dry sherry
Water—barely enough to cover ingredients
1 tablespoon cornstarch in 2 tablespoons cold water (optional)

Brown the garlic, ginger, pork, and chicken in 2 tablespoons of cooking oil over medium-high heat. Add soy sauce, sugar, sherry, and sufficient water to cover meat.

Cover and simmer over low heat for about an hour or until meat is tender. Remove ginger and garlic clove. Serve meat hot with the sauce. If you wish, the sauce may be thickened by adding 1 tablespoon of cornstarch in 2 tablespoons of cold water to the sauce. Heat until the sauce thickens and is clear.

chapter 7
soups

peking egg drop soup

Yield: 4 to 6 servings

¼ pound lean pork shoulder, cut
    into fine strips
2 ounces bamboo shoots, finely
    sliced
4 or 5 dried black Chinese
    mushrooms, soaked 30
    minutes in warm water and
    cut into small pieces
2 tablespoons vinegar
2 teaspoons soy sauce
¼ teaspoon (or less) ground
    pepper
1 quart chicken broth
½ teaspoon salt (or salt to taste)
1½ tablespoons cornstarch in 2
    tablespoons water
1 egg, beaten

peking egg drop soup

Brown the strips of pork well in the wok or in a large saucepan. Add bamboo shoots, mushrooms, vinegar, soy sauce, pepper, chicken broth, salt, and cornstarch mixture. Bring mixture to a full boil, stirring constantly. Reduce heat. Add egg, a small amount at a time, stirring with a fork to separate it into shreds as it coagulates. Remove from heat and serve at once.

chicken egg drop soup

Yield: 4 servings

6 cups chicken broth
2 tablespoons cornstarch in 2
    tablespoons water
1 tablespoon soy sauce
½ teaspoon sugar

2 eggs, lightly beaten
Salt and pepper
2 scallions, sliced (green tops
    included)

Bring the chicken broth to a boil. Combine the cornstarch mixture with the soy sauce and sugar. Slowly stir into the broth. Heat and continue stirring until the soup is thickened and clear. Remove from the heat. Gradually add eggs, stirring with a fork until eggs separate into shreds. Season to taste with salt and pepper. Serve immediately garnished with sliced scallions.

clam soup

Yield: 3 or 4 servings

1 dozen large, fresh clams
5 cups water
1 teaspoon salt

1 teaspoon soy sauce
2 tablespoons dry sherry
1 scallion, sliced

Scrub the clams with a stiff brush to remove all sand and debris. Drop the clams into boiling water and boil just until the shells have opened. Remove from heat and discard the shells. Add the salt, soy sauce, and dry sherry to the broth. Place 3 or 4 clams in each bowl. Add the broth, and garnish with scallion slices.

hot-and-sour soup

Yield: 4 to 6 servings

3 cups chicken broth
⅓ pound lean pork, shredded into
    matchstick-size pieces
4 Chinese dried black mushrooms,
    soaked for 20 to 30 minutes in
    warm water, and sliced
2 ounces bean curd, cut into
    matchstick-size pieces

2 tablespoons soy sauce
2 tablespoons dry sherry
1 teaspoon salt
½ teaspoon pepper
2 tablespoons vinegar
1 tablespoon cornstarch in 2
    tablespoons cold water

Bring the broth to a boil in the wok and add the pork, mushrooms, and bean curd. Simmer for 8 minutes, until the pork is done. Add the soy sauce, sherry, salt, pepper, vinegar, and the cornstarch mixture. Continue to heat until the soup has thickened. Serve hot.

corn and chicken soup

Yield: 4 to 6 servings

6 ounces raw chicken meat,
    minced
1 tablespoon dry sherry
1 teaspoon salt
2 egg whites

1 quart chicken broth
1 10-ounce can cream-style corn
2 tablespoons cornstarch in ¼ cup
    cold water
Thin strips of ham

Combine the chicken with the sherry, salt, and egg whites. Bring the chicken broth to a full, rolling boil. Add minced-chicken mixture and corn. Simmer 2 minutes. Add cornstarch mixture and simmer an additional 2 minutes, stirring continuously. Add more salt, if needed. Pour into serving bowls and garnish with thin strips of ham.

corn and chicken soup

bird's nest soup

Yield: 8 servings

1½ cups bird's nest soaked overnight in 1 quart of water, feathers and debris removed

1½ pounds chicken (including bones)

6 cups cold water
4 teaspoons salt
5 dried red dates, if desired
½ cup cooked ham, chopped fine

Cook the bird's nest and water slowly for 1 hour in a wok and drain off the water. Cold water may be added to cool the bird's nest. Take a small portion of the bird's nest in the hand and squeeze out the excess water; remove and discard the black and brown particles. Look over the entire quantity in this manner.

Place the chicken in 6 cups cold water, add the salt, and skim off the substance that rises to the top as the liquid comes to the boiling point. Cook slowly for 1½ hours. Add the dates and cleaned bird's nest and continue simmering for 3 to 4 hours. Remove the chicken, separate the meat from the bones, and chop the meat fine. Add 1 cup chopped chicken and ½ cup chopped ham to the soup.

Mix slightly and serve hot. This soup is usually served as the first course of a banquet or elaborate dinner.

imitation bird's nest or long-rice soup

Yield: 6 to 8 servings

1 cup soaked long rice (½ bunch—available in Oriental-food stores)
¾ teaspoon salt
5 cups boiling water or chicken broth
⅜ cup finely minced fresh lean pork
⅓ cup finely minced smoked ham
1 tablespoon finely chopped water chestnuts

½ tablespoon soy sauce
1 teaspoon (or ½ cup, optional) finely chopped green onions (with tops)
½ cup finely chopped mushrooms (optional)
½ cup finely chopped bamboo shoots (optional)
¼ teaspoon cornstarch (optional)

Soak the long rice in cold water for ½ hour. Drain, and cut in 6-inch lengths. Add long rice and salt to the boiling water and boil for 20 minutes. Combine the pork, ham, water chestnuts, and soy sauce. Shape into balls ¾ inch in diameter. Drop into the soup mixture and boil 10 minutes. Do not stir. Add the green onions and serve immediately. To improve the flavor, ½ cup finely chopped mushrooms and ½ cup finely chopped bamboo shoots may be added to the soup and the green onions increased to ½ cup.

One-fourth teaspoon cornstarch may be mixed with the soy sauce and meat mixture so that the balls will retain their shape during cooking.

pork and watercress soup

Yield: 4 to 6 servings

½ pound lean pork, shredded
6 cups chicken broth
1 small onion, sliced thin
1 celery stalk, sliced thin
1 teaspoon salt

¼ teaspoon pepper
1 cup firmly packed washed
    watercress, cut into 1-inch
    pieces

Simmer the pork in the chicken broth for 10 minutes. Add the onion, celery, salt, and pepper and simmer for 10 minutes longer. Add the watercress and heat briefly.

chinese soup

Yield: 4 to 6 servings

1 quart chicken broth
½ teaspoon salt (or salt to taste)
¼ teaspoon pepper (or less)
2 teaspoons soy sauce
2 ounces whole, cooked shrimps

2 ounces cooked ham, cut into thin
    strips
2 ounces cooked chicken, cut into
    thin strips

Bring the chicken broth to a boil and add all the remaining ingredients. Simmer 3 to 4 minutes and serve immediately.

chinese soup

celery cabbage and shrimp soup

Yield: 6 servings

1 small head celery cabbage
5 water chestnuts
½ cup large dried or 1 cup canned
shrimps
1 cup water
1 tablespoon vegetable oil
3½ cups boiling water
1 teaspoon salt
4 green onions (with tops), finely
chopped

Wash and cut the cabbage crosswise into 1-inch strips. Wash, peel, and cut the water chestnuts crosswise into ¼-inch slices. Soak the dried shrimps in 1 cup water for ½ hour. Drain the shrimps, but save the liquid. Heat the oil until it is very hot, add the shrimps, and fry for 2 to 3 minutes. Add the shrimp liquid, water chestnuts, 3½ cups boiling water, and salt. Bring the liquid to the boiling point and simmer for ½ hour. Add the cabbage and boil for 5 to 10 minutes, until the cabbage is tender but has not lost all its crispness. Add the finely chopped green onions and serve hot.

If wet-packed shrimps are used, substitute ⅔ cup liquid from the canned shrimps for ⅔ cup water. Clean the shrimps by removing the black vein along the back.

celery cabbage and pork soup

Yield: 6 servings

1 small head celery cabbage
5 water chestnuts
4 green onions (with tops), very
finely chopped
½ cup ground pork
1 egg yolk
¾ teaspoon salt
4 cups boiling water

Wash and cut the cabbage crosswise into 1½-inch strips. Wash, peel, and cut the water chestnuts in cross sections ¼ inch thick. Chop the onions very fine and mix with the pork. Add the egg yolk. Combine the salt, boiling water, and water chestnuts; cook for 15 minutes. Add the cabbage and cook until it is nearly tender. Drop the pork mixture, a teaspoonful at a time, into the soup. Boil for 5 minutes and serve hot.

cucumber soup

Yield: 6 servings

¾ tablespoon salt
¼ teaspoon cornstarch
1 teaspoon soy sauce
½ cup pork, sliced in pieces ½ x ¼ x ¾ inch
1 tablespoon vegetable oil
4 cups water

10 medium-size mushrooms, cut into ½-inch strips
5 red dates, if desired
¾ cup bamboo shoots, sliced in pieces ½ x ¼ x ¾ inch
3 cucumbers
Fish balls (optional)

Add ¼ teaspoon salt, cornstarch, and soy sauce to the pork and allow them to stand for 5 minutes. Heat the oil and brown the pork for 3 minutes. Add the water, mushrooms, red dates, bamboo shoots, and remaining salt, and simmer for 30 to 45 minutes. Discard the red dates. Peel the cucumbers and cut them into cross sections. Add the cucumber pieces to the soup and boil it for 3 minutes. Serve immediately.

Fish balls may be added. Drop them into the boiling soup and boil for 3 minutes after they come to the surface. Then add the cucumber pieces and boil the soup for 3 minutes.

green mustard cabbage and dried shrimp soup

Yield: 6 servings

1 bunch green mustard cabbage (¾ pound), cut crosswise into 1½-inch pieces
½ cup large dried shrimps
4½ cups water
1 tablespoon vegetable oil
1 teaspoon salt

Keep the cabbage leaf and stalk pieces separate. Wash and soak the dried shrimps in 1 cup water for ½ hour. Drain the shrimps but save the liquid. Add the shrimps to very hot oil and fry them for 2 or 3 minutes. Add the remaining water and the shrimp liquid and simmer for ½ hour. Add the cabbage stalks and boil them for 1 minute; add the leaves, and boil for 2 minutes. Serve the soup immediately.

Finely sliced lean pork or beef may be substituted for the shrimps. Combine ½ cup meat with water or soup, add salt, and simmer for ½ hour. Add the cabbage with stalks and leaves separated. Watercress, celery cabbage, or spinach may be substituted for mustard cabbage.

watercress soup

Yield: 5 servings

4 cups watercress, cut in 2-inch
  pieces
4½ cups water

1 teaspoon salt
¼ cup fresh lean pork, sliced 1½ x
  ½ x ¼ inches

Wash the watercress thoroughly and discard the tough stems. Cut the watercress and keep the tougher portions separate. Combine the water, salt, and pork and simmer for 30 minutes. Add the tough watercress and boil for 1 minute. Add the watercress tips, boil for 1 minute, and serve immediately.

chicken soup

Yield: 4 to 6 servings

2 5-ounce cans boned chicken
5 cups chicken broth (use the
     liquid from the boned
     chicken as part of this liquid)
1 4-ounce can mushroom stems
     and pieces, drained and
     liquid reserved
2 teaspoons soy sauce
2 cups fine egg noodles
4 thin slices lemon with rind

Add the chicken to the broth in the wok. Cover and bring slowly to a boil. Add the mushrooms, soy sauce, and noodles. Stir and cook until the noodles are done. Garnish with lemon rind.

lotus root and pork soup

Yield: 6 servings

1 pound lotus root (4 sections)
5 cups cold water
1 pound soup bone (with very
     little meat)
⅓ pound lean pork
1½ teaspoons salt

Place the scraped lotus root in cold water. Bring the water to a boil, add the soup bone and piece of pork, and simmer for 3 to 4 hours. Add the salt near the end of the cooking period. Remove the lotus root and pork. Cut them into thin slices, place in a serving dish, and pour in the soup stock.

The lotus root and pork may also be served separately and the soup served clear.

noodle soup

Yield: 8 servings

1 box Canton or egg noodles (14 ounces)
2 eggs
½ tablespoon vegetable oil
5 medium dried mushrooms or ½ cup canned mushrooms
½ roll salted mustard cabbage root, if desired
5 cups meat, abalone, or chicken stock
1 tablespoon salt
3 tablespoons soy sauce
2 green onions, chopped fine
2 large pieces canned abalone
½ pound roast pork
Soy sauce and oil

Cook the noodles in salted boiling water for 15 minutes. Drain, and set them aside. Beat the eggs slightly. Heat the oil in a wok. Fry the eggs in one thin layer for 1 to 2 minutes or until firm. Turn over once. Fry for 1 minute. Remove from the wok and allow to cool.

Soak the dried mushrooms in water for 20 to 30 minutes. Drain mushrooms, remove, and discard the stems. Wash the salted cabbage root 3 or 4 times with cold water. Add the cabbage root and mushrooms to the stock and boil slowly for 45 minutes. Add the salt, soy sauce, and onions. Simmer for 2 to 3 minutes and remove the mushrooms.

Cut mushrooms, abalone, roast pork, and fried eggs into narrow strips about 1½ inches long and ⅛ inch wide. Place the noodles in a serving bowl. Spread the abalone over the noodles, then add the mushrooms, roast pork, and eggs. When ready to eat, pour the hot soup over this. Season at the table with the following mixture of soy sauce and oil.

sauce

1 tablespoon peanut or vegetable oil
¼ cup soy sauce
Combine the peanut oil and soy sauce and heat in a saucepan.

spinach soup with pork

Yield: 6 servings

1½ bunches spinach (1½ pounds)
1 tablespoon soy sauce
2¼ teaspoons salt
½ cup sliced lean pork, sliced 1½
    x ½ x ¼ inches
1 tablespoon vegetable oil
1 clove garlic, mashed
6 cups boiling water

Remove the tough stems from the spinach and wash the leafy portions thoroughly. Add the soy sauce and ¼ teaspoon salt to the pork. Heat the oil in a wok, add the mashed garlic and pork, and fry them for 3 minutes. Remove the garlic if desired. Add the boiling water, 2 teaspoons salt, and simmer for 10 minutes. Add the spinach and simmer for 5 minutes. Serve hot.

One-fourth cup dried shrimps may be substituted for the pork and the salt reduced to 1½ teaspoons. Wash and soak the shrimps for 15 minutes. Drain, but keep the liquid. Fry the shrimps, add the liquid, and simmer for 10 minutes, then add the spinach.

fig and pork soup

Yield: 8 servings

1 pound partially ripe figs
4 dried red dates, if desired
¼ roll salted mustard cabbage
    root, if desired
¼ pound pork liver
1 pound pork soup bone (with
    very little meat)
½ pound lean pork
5 cups boiling water
1½ teaspoons salt

Remove stem ends, wash, and cut the figs into quarters. Wash red dates and cabbage root. Remove white tissue from the liver. Combine all the ingredients and boil slowly for 1½ hours.

Remove the liver and pork and slice them into strips. Discard red dates, cabbage root, and the soup bone. Serve the figs and soup in a bowl garnished with slices of pork and liver.

chapter 8
other recipes

foil-wrapped beef

Yield: 4 servings

1 pound beef (top of the round or chuck blade steak or roast), very thinly sliced (partial freezing may make this step easier)

2 tablespoons hoisin sauce

1 tablespoon soy sauce
1 tablespoon dry sherry
1 tablespoon cornstarch
4 12-inch aluminum foil squares
1 scallion, finely sliced
Parsley leaves

Combine the beef, hoisin sauce, soy sauce, dry sherry, and cornstarch. Place one-fourth of this mixture in a single layer in the center of each foil square. Top each with sliced scallion and parsley leaves. (You can divide the mixture into smaller portions and make 6 to 8 squares.) Fold as for Paper-Wrapped chicken into flat packages about 5 inches square. Keeping the seams up to prevent the escape of juices, bake at 450°F for 6 minutes. Serve still wrapped so the diner can release the flavorful juices at the moment of eating. (It is important to wrap in a single layer in a flat package or the beef will not be uniformly cooked.) A delicious, unique way to serve beef!

adele's won ton rolls

Yield: 16 rolls

⅓ cup orange marmalade
1 tablespoon lemon juice
2 tablespoons soy sauce

2 tablespoons margarine
½ cup cornflake crumbs
2 tubes crescent rolls

Combine all ingredients except the rolls. Open the rolls and separate them into triangles. Spoon some of the marmalade mixture into the center of each triangle. Stretch and fold the points up around the filling, shaping the roll into a pocket. Place on greased cookie sheets and bake at 400°F for 10 minutes. Serve warm with Oriental meals.

chicken bits oriental

Yield: 3 to 4 servings

2 tablespoons vegetable oil
2 whole chicken breasts, boned
    and cubed
¼ cup chicken bouillon
3 tablespoons sherry
1 tablespoon soy sauce
½ teaspoon ginger
½ cup water chestnuts, drained
    and sliced thin

¼ cup bamboo shoots, sliced thin
½ cup pineapple chunks, drained
1 cup frozen peas
3 tablespoons reserved pineapple
    liquid
2 teaspoons cornstarch
2 tablespoons hoisin sauce
1 tablespoon scallion, minced

Heat vegetable oil in a wok. Add chicken cubes and sauté over high heat until evenly browned.

Add the chicken bouillon, sherry, soy sauce, ginger, water chestnuts, bamboo shoots, pineapple chunks, and peas. Stir to mix well, then cook over medium heat, stirring constantly, for 2 minutes.

Mix the pineapple liquid and cornstarch together well. Add to the chicken mixture. Add the hoisin sauce, mix all well, and cook, stirring constantly, until sauce thickens. Sprinkle on the scallions before serving.

chinese rolls

Yield: Approximately 4 servings

1 pound lean pork shoulder, ham,
    or beef, cut into slices
1 teaspoon salt
¼ teaspoon pepper
½ to 1 tablespoon aniseed
2 tablespoons butter or margarine
    for frying
Juice from 1 large orange
1 tablespoon soy sauce
3 to 4 tablespoons chili sauce

Flatten the meat slices on a cutting board and season them with salt, pepper, and aniseed. Roll up the slices and fasten with a toothpick. Brown the rolls all around in browned butter or margarine and transfer them to a wok. Boil a few tablespoons of water in the frying pan and pour the gravy over the rolls. Add orange juice and soy sauce, bring to a boil, and let rolls simmer under cover for 25 to 30 minutes. Add the chili sauce toward the end of the cooking period. Serve with boiled rice.

122

peking duck

Yield: Approximately 6 servings

4- to 5-pound duck
6 cups water
¼ cup honey
4 slices peeled fresh ginger root,
about 1 inch in diameter and
⅛ inch thick
2 scallions, including the green
tops, cut into 2 inch lengths
12 scallion brushes
Mandarin pancakes

sauce

¼ cup hoisin sauce
1 tablespoon water
1 teaspoon sesame seed oil
2 teaspoons sugar

Wash the duck thoroughly with cold water, and dry. Tie a cord tightly around the neck skin and suspend the bird in an airy place to dry the skin (about 3 hours).

Bring to a boil in a wok 6 cups of water, ¼ cup honey, ginger root, and cut scallions. Lower the duck by its string into the boiling liquid and use a spoon to moisten the duck's skin thoroughly. Discard the liquid and suspend the duck by its cord until it is dry (2 to 3 hours).

Make the sauce by combining hoisin sauce, water, sesame seed oil, and sugar in a small pan, and stir until the sugar dissolves. Bring to a boil and then simmer, uncovered, for 3 minutes. Cool and save for later use.

Cut scallions to 3 inch lengths and trim off the roots. Standing each scallion on end, make 4 intersecting cuts 1 inch deep into its stalk. Repeat at other end. Place scallions in ice water and refrigerate until cut parts curl into brushlike fans.

Preheat oven to 375°F. Untie the duck and cut off any loose neck skin. Place duck, breast side up, on a rack and set in a roasting pan. Roast the duck for 1 hour. Lower the heat to 300°F, turn the duck on its breast, and roast for 30 minutes longer. Raise the heat to 375°F, return the duck to its back, and roast for a final 30 minutes. Transfer the duck to a carving board.

With a small, sharp knife and your fingers, remove the crisp skin from the breast, sides, and back of the duck. Cut the skin into 2- by 3-inch rectangles and arrange them in a single layer on a platter. Cut the wings and drumsticks from the duck, and cut all the meat away from the breast and carcass. Slice the meat into pieces 2½ inches long and ½ inch wide, and arrange them on another platter.

Serve the duck with Mandarin pancakes, sauce, and the scallion brushes. Dip a scallion brush into the sauce and brush a pancake with it. The scallion is placed in the middle of the pancake with a piece of duck skin and a piece of meat. The pancake is rolled around the pieces and eaten like a sandwich. The mixture of flavors is exquisite.

almond-sprinkled pork stew

Yield: Approximately 4 servings

1 pound sliced pork shoulder	1 green and 1 red paprika
½ teaspoon paprika powder	1 cup grated celery root
1 teaspoon curry	1 grated apple (not sweet)
2 tablespoons flour	½ cup almonds
2 cups bouillon	Soy sauce
2 onions	

Cut pork in fine strips and brown slightly in a wok. Turn over to casserole. Sprinkle paprika powder, curry, and flour over the pork and hot bouillon while stirring briskly. Brown small wedges of onion, strips of paprika, celery, and apple in the frying pan and add to pork. Cook on slow heat or simmer tightly covered for about 25 minutes. Add liquid, if necessary, and season to taste. Halve the almonds and brown slightly in a small amount of oil. Serve with soy sauce over rice.

almond-sprinkled pork stew

javanese spiced pork

Yield: Approximately 6 servings

1½ pounds boneless pork
2 large yellow onions
1 teaspoon coriander
1 teaspoon curry
1 teaspoon salt
½ teaspoon freshly ground black
   pepper

2 medium pressed clove garlics
1 tablespoon soy sauce
¾ cup shelled and deveined
   shrimps
3 eggs

sauce

4 tablespoons peanut butter
3 tablespoons milk
2 tablespoons soy sauce

½ to 1½ teaspoons Tabasco sauce
1 teaspoon corn syrup

Cut the pork into very thin slices. Peel and finely chop the onions. Brown the pork and onion in some oil in the wok, cover, and continue to fry on very low heat for 10 minutes. Add the coriander, curry, salt, black pepper, garlic, and soy sauce. Mix thoroughly. Let fry slowly for another 10 minutes. Add the shrimps and let them get warm. Meanwhile, beat the eggs and stir them into the wok. Let simmer for 1 minute and remove from the heat. Serve with boiled rice and the special sauce.

Sauce: Beat the peanut butter rapidly with the milk and soy sauce. Keep these ingredients cold. Add the Tabasco sauce and the corn syrup. Beer makes an excellent companion beverage.

javanese spiced pork

oriental pork loin

Yield: About 4 servings

2 pounds pork loin
1 red and 1 green pepper
½ teaspoon curry powder
½ teaspoon paprika powder
3 tablespoons vegetable oil
3 tablespoons flour
1 cup bouillon
½ cup milk

½ cup cream
1 small can of vegetable juice
Salt
Garlic powder
1 tablespoon mango chutney
2 tablespoons dry white wine (if
    desired)

Cut the meat into strips and the peppers into small pieces. Brown the curry and paprika in the vegetable oil until pungent. Add, while stirring in the wok, the flour, bouillon, milk, and cream. Add the juice, meat, and the diced peppers. Simmer for about 5 minutes. Add water, if needed, spices, mango, and wine. Serve with almonds and rice.

oriental pork loin

oriental pork stew

Yield: 4 servings

**1 pound cooked pork, cut into
   bite-size pieces**
1 leek or 2 scallions, sliced
**1 small head of cabbage, sliced
   into ¼-inch slices**

marinade

2 tablespoons vegetable oil
2 tablespoons soy sauce
1 teaspoon grated ginger
½ teaspoon garlic salt
**8- to 10-ounce can pineapple slices
   (4 or 5 slices), cut into pieces**
**Syrup from drained pineapple
   slices**

oriental pork stew

Combine the ingredients for the marinade in a small bowl. Add pork, cover, and marinate a few hours in the refrigerator. Pour the meat and marinade into the wok or saucepan. Add the scallions and cabbage. Simmer for 30 minutes. Serve with boiled rice.

mandarin pancakes

Yield: About 24 pancakes

2 cups sifted all-purpose flour
¾ cup boiling water
1 to 2 tablespoons sesame seed oil

Prepare a well in the sifted flour and pour the water into it. Mix and knead the dough for 10 minutes. Let it rest for 15 minutes under a damp kitchen towel. Roll to a thickness of about ¼ inch with a rolling pin. Stamp out circles 2½ inches in diameter with a cookie cutter or a glass.

Brush half of the circles lightly with the sesame seed oil. Place an unoiled circle on top of an oiled one and roll flat to a diameter of about 6 inches. Fry each pancake, 1 minute to a side, in an unoiled skillet. As each pancake is finished, gently separate the halves and stack them. These are traditionally served with Peking duck.

eggs with bean sprouts

Yield: 4 servings

2 tablespoons vegetable oil
2 scallions, cut into ¼-inch slices
2 ounces mushrooms, cut into "T"
    shapes
4 eggs
3 water chestnuts, cut into thin
    slices
3 ounces cooked chicken meat,
    shredded
1 tablespoon soy sauce
½ teaspoon sugar
½ teaspoon salt
½ tomato, cut into thin wedges
1 cup bean sprouts

sauce
    ¾ cup water
    1½ teaspoons cornstarch
    1½ teaspoons sugar
    1 tablespoon soy sauce

Heat the oil in the wok and stir-fry the scallions and mushrooms 1 to 2 minutes. Combine the eggs, water chestnuts, chicken, soy sauce, sugar, and salt. Add to the scallions and mushrooms in the wok and stir briefly. After the eggs have heated for about a minute, spread the tomato wedges and bean sprouts over the top. Continue cooking until the eggs are browned on the bottom. Do not stir. Carefully turn the eggs over and cook for another minute. Slide the omelette out onto a hot dish and serve with the thickened soy sauce prepared by combining all ingredients and bringing to a boil, stirring continuously. Serve at once.

eggs foo young

Yield: 4 servings

2 tablespoons vegetable oil
½ cup thinly sliced scallions
¼ cup celery, finely chopped
1 clove garlic, crushed
1 cup cooked shrimps or pork,
    diced
6 eggs
½ teaspoon salt
¼ teaspoon pepper
1 tablespoon soy sauce

Heat the oil in the wok. Add scallions, celery, and garlic, and stir-fry 2 to 3 minutes. Remove and discard the garlic. Add the shrimps and continue to stir-fry until shrimps are lightly browned. Beat the eggs with the salt, pepper, and soy sauce until frothy. Add to the shrimp mixture and stir until blended. Cook over low heat until the eggs set. Fold over and slide onto serving plate. Serve at once.

mushroom omelette

Yield: 4 servings

2 tablespoons butter
¼ cup mushrooms, sliced
¼ cup finely chopped onions
6 eggs
Salt and pepper
Lettuce or parsley for garnish

Melt butter in wok, and, over a very low heat, stir-fry the mushrooms and onions. (Butter will burn if heated over 225°F.) Remove and set aside. Beat eggs with salt and pepper. Pour into wok and heat slowly. Lift up edges of the eggs as they become set on the bottom and allow uncooked egg to run under. Cook until golden brown on bottom and creamy on top. Place mushrooms and onions in center and roll out on plate. Garnish with lettuce or parsley. Serve at once.

watercress omelette

Yield: 2 servings

3 eggs
1 tablespoon water
½ teaspoon salt
2 tablespoons finely chopped
**   watercress**
2 tablespoons melted butter or
**   margarine**
2 tablespoons grated process
**   Gruyère cheese**
2 tablespoons diced cooked bacon
**   or ham**
3 tablespoons diced peeled
**   tomato, or 6 to 8 cherry**
**   tomatoes, halved**
Freshly grated pepper
Watercress (garnish)

Mix eggs and water slightly. Stir in salt and chopped watercress. Place the wok over heat for a few minutes. Add butter or margarine; when it sizzles, add egg mixture and stir rapidly with a fork until mixture begins to set. Sprinkle cheese, bacon or ham, and tomatoes on top. Lower heat.

When omelette is set, loosen edges, and fold over in half. Slide onto a warm plate. Sprinkle with pepper and garnish with watercress. Serve.

You can repeat this process at the table for any desired number of omelettes. Have the egg mixture ready with bowls of grated cheese, bacon or ham, and tomato.

oriental shrimp

Yield: Approximately 4 servings

1 teaspoon curry and, perhaps,
  some paprika powder
4 tablespoons margarine or butter
2 red and 2 green paprikas
2 yellow onions or 2 pieces of leek
2 clove garlics or garlic powder
2 pounds shelled and deveined
  shrimps

6 tablespoons tomato purée
½ cup water
½ cup dry white wine
½ cup heavy cream
Salt
2 cups fresh mushrooms

In a wok fry the curry and paprika powder in the margarine or butter, add paprika strips, onions, garlic, and shrimps to soften. Add the tomato purée, water, wine, and cream and let simmer for a few minutes. Heat the shrimps in the mixture, taste, and correct seasoning. Stir in the mushrooms and finish cooking.

This mixture can be served hot in shells or eaten with white bread or rice. The mixture can also be used as filling in crepes.

oriental shrimp

ground beef oriental

Yield: 3 to 4 servings

1 tablespoon vegetable oil
1 pound ground chuck or ground
    round
1 small onion or 2 scallions,
    chopped
1 clove garlic, crushed
½ teaspoon salt

¼ teaspoon pepper
¾ cup beef bouillon
½ green pepper, cut in thin strips
1 fresh tomato, cut in eighths
¼ cup bamboo shoots, sliced thin *
1½ tablespoons soy sauce
½ teaspoon cornstarch

Heat vegetable oil in a wok. When hot, add the ground beef, onion, garlic, salt, and pepper. Stir with a fork, breaking up beef into small pieces, and sauté until beef is browned and onion soft. Pour off any fat that accumulates.

Pour in bouillon, and add green pepper, tomato, and bamboo shoots. Bring mixture to a boil. Mix soy sauce and cornstarch together, and add. Cook over low heat, stirring occasionally, until sauce thickens.

*Bamboo shoots are available canned in most supermarkets and in Chinese grocery stores.

chinese beef

Yield: 4 to 6 servings

½ cup dried Chinese mushrooms
1½ pounds flank steak
2 small tomatoes, peeled *
1 green pepper
2 tablespoons olive oil
1 clove garlic, crushed
1 teaspoon salt
Dash pepper

¼ teaspoon ginger
3 tablespoons soy sauce
2 tablespoons sherry
½ teaspoon sugar
1 1-pound can bean sprouts,
    drained
1 tablespoon cornstarch
3 tablespoons water

Soak Chinese mushrooms in water to cover for 20 minutes. Drain and halve large mushrooms. Cut flank steaks in strips across grain (about 2 x 1 x ¼ inches). Cut tomatoes in eighths. Cut green pepper in 1-inch cubes.

Heat the oil in a large skillet or wok. Add the flank steak strips, garlic, salt, pepper, and ginger. Sauté over high heat until the meat is evenly browned on all sides. Add the soy sauce, sherry, sugar, tomatoes, green pepper, mushrooms, and bean sprouts. Stir until well-mixed, cover, and cook over medium heat for 5 minutes.

Make a paste of the cornstarch and water and add to the beef mixture. Cook, uncovered, stirring occasionally, until sauce thickens.

*Tomatoes can be peeled easily by dipping in boiling water for a few seconds or by holding directly over a flame for a few seconds. (If the second method is used, be sure fork used to hold tomato has a wooden handle.)

chinese style lamb

Yield: About 4 servings

2-pound boneless leg of lamb
Salt and pepper
2 tablespoons vegetable oil
1 small, sliced onion
2 large carrots, sliced
1 tablespoon corn syrup
3 tablespoons tomato catsup

1 tablespoon soy sauce or
    Worcestershire sauce
1 tablespoon juice from pineapple
    rings
8-ounce can pineapple rings
1 bunch spring onions

Remove and discard excess fat from the meat. Cut the meat into 1-inch cubes. Season well with salt and pepper.

Heat the oil in a wok. Gently fry the lamb, onion, and sliced carrots until golden. Add the syrup, catsup, soy or Worcestershire sauce, and 1 tablespoon of juice from the pineapple rings.

Drain the pineapple rings and cut them in half.

Wash the spring onions and cut off some of the green part.

Cover pan with tightly fitting lid and simmer very gently for 45 minutes or until the lamb is very tender. Add the pineapple and spring onions about 5 minutes before the end of cooking time. Serve with boiled rice, mixed with peas, plain rice, and, if you like, bean sprouts.

chinese style lamb

javanese chicken casserole

Yield: Approximately 4 servings

2 pounds chicken breasts
1 pound chicken livers
1½ teaspoons flour
Salt and pepper
3 tablespoons margarine or butter
1 pound small onions

1 green paprika
½ can bamboo sprouts
3 to 4 slices of canned pineapple
1 teaspoon ginger
2 teaspoons brown sugar
2 teaspoons wine vinegar

Cut the chicken breasts into even pieces. Do the same with the livers. Coat breast and liver pieces in the flour combined with salt and pepper. Brown the pieces in a little more than half of the margarine or butter in a wok. Transfer to a casserole. Brown the onions in the rest of the melted fat, allowing the paprika to fry with the onions for a few minutes, then transfer all to the casserole. Whisk the wok with some water and pour into casserole. Add well-drained bamboo sprouts, slices of pineapple, and seasonings. Simmer the dish under cover for about 20 minutes. Meanwhile boil rice to be served with the dish. Beer or red wine is a good beverage with this dish.

javanese chicken casserole

chapter 9
hors d'oeuvres

barbequed pork

Yield: 8 to 12 servings as an appetizer

1 clove garlic	½ teaspoon red food coloring
2 slices fresh ginger root	2 scallions, sliced thin
3 tablespoons brown sugar	¼ cup chicken stock
2 tablespoons dry sherry	2 pounds lean pork butt or
4 tablespoons soy sauce	shoulder, boned and sliced
½ teaspoon 5-spices powder	into 2-inch-thick slices

Combine all the ingredients except the pork and bring to a simmering temperature. Place the pork in a shallow bowl and cover with the warmed marinade. Cover and refrigerate overnight. Turn the slices occasionally to be sure all have equal exposure to the marinade. Remove pork and place on a rack over a dripping pan. Baste well with the marinade. Roast in a 325°F oven for 1½ hours, basting often with the marinade and drippings. To serve warm, cut the thick slices into ⅛-inch-thin slices and arrange on a platter. Pour over some of the warm marinade. To serve cold, allow the meat to cool in the marinade, slice thinly, and serve with or without the marinade as a sauce. Serve as an appetizer or in sandwiches.

oriental cocktail kebabs

Yield: 40 to 50

1 15¼-ounce can pineapple
    chunks, drained
1-pound package
    brown-and-serve sausages,
    cooked according to the
    package directions, and cut
    into thirds
1 8-ounce can water chestnuts,
    halved
2 green peppers, cut into ¾-inch
    squares
¼ pound small mushrooms,
    stemmed
Reserved syrup from drained
    pineapple
4 tablespoons soy sauce
3 slices fresh ginger root
3 tablespoons brown sugar
2 tablespoons dry sherry

Alternate pieces of pineapple, sausage, water chestnuts, green pepper, and mushrooms on toothpicks. Combine the reserved pineapple syrup, soy sauce, ginger root, brown sugar, and sherry and heat in a skillet. Add the kebabs, cover, and simmer 10 minutes. Remove from skillet and serve warm.

stuffed mushrooms

Yield: 12 appetizers

8 ounces cooked crab, shrimp, or
    lobster, minced
4 water chestnuts, minced
1 scallion, minced
2 teaspoons soy sauce
1 teaspoon dry sherry
1 teaspoon sugar

1 teaspoon cornstarch
1 egg
12 mushroom stems, minced and
    browned in a little oil
12 large mushrooms, stems
    removed
Parsley (optional)

Combine the minced crab, chestnuts, and scallion with the remaining ingredients. Fill the mushroom caps with the mixture and bake at 350°F for 20 minutes. Serve hot garnished with parsley.

shrimp puffs

Yield: About 16

1 pound shrimps, cleaned,
   deveined, chopped very fine
8 to 9 water chestnuts, minced
1 egg, beaten
1 teaspoon salt
½ teaspoon sugar

1 teaspoon cornstarch
2 teaspoons dry sherry
1 teaspoon soy sauce
2 cups oil for frying
Lemon wedges and soy sauce for
   dipping

Combine the shrimps, water chestnuts, egg, salt, sugar, cornstarch, sherry, and soy sauce. Heat oil in the wok to 375°F. Shape the shrimp mixture into balls the size of small walnuts and drop from a spoon into the hot oil. Fry until the balls float and turn pink and golden. Drain on paper towels. Serve hot with lemon wedges and a bowl of soy sauce for dipping.

marinated radishes and celery

4 tablespoons soy sauce
6 tablespoons vinegar
1 tablespoon sesame oil
6-ounce bag radishes, cleaned
2 stalks celery, sliced diagonally
   into 1-inch pieces

Mix soy sauce, vinegar, and sesame oil in small bowl. Add radishes and celery. Cover and refrigerate 1 hour—no longer.

water chestnuts with bacon

Yield: About 20

⅓ to ½ pound bacon
1 6-ounce can of water chestnuts
Toothpicks
1 tablespoon soy sauce
1 tablespoon dry sherry

Wrap ½ slice of bacon around each water chestnut and fasten with a toothpick. Place the water chestnuts in an oven-proof dish and brush with a mixture of soy sauce and sherry. Bake at 350°F for 15 to 20 minutes.

sari's hong kong meatballs

Yield: 6 servings

1½ pounds ground beef
½ cup celery, very finely chopped
1 teaspoon seasoned salt
1 teaspoon soy sauce
1 tablespoon vegetable oil
¼ cup bamboo shoots, sliced thin
1 1-pound can mixed Chinese
    vegetables or bean sprouts,
    drained, with liquid reserved
1 green pepper, seeded and cut in
    julienne strips
1 carrot, peeled and shredded
1 5-ounce can water chestnuts,
    drained and sliced thin
1½ tablespoons cornstarch
2 teaspoons (additional) soy sauce
2 teaspoons sherry
¼ cup blanched, slivered almonds

Mix ground beef with celery, seasoned salt, and soy sauce. Mix thoroughly to blend all ingredients, then shape into 1-inch-diameter meatballs.

Heat the vegetable oil in a large skillet or wok, and sauté the meatballs over high heat until browned on all sides. Stir in the bamboo shoots; cover, and simmer 5 minutes, stirring occasionally. At the end of the cooking time, pour off any accumulated fat.

Add the drained Chinese vegetables, green pepper strips, shredded carrot, and water chestnuts. Stir well. In a 2-cup measure, mix the cornstarch, soy sauce, and sherry until a thin paste is formed. Add the liquid from the Chinese vegetables and enough water to make 2 cups in all. Add to the meatballs and cook uncovered for 5 to 10 minutes, stirring occasionally, until sauce is thickened. Sprinkle on the almonds before serving.

chapter 10
desserts

spun-sugar fruit dessert

Yield: 4 servings

assorted fruits to serve 4

**Apples, peeled, cored, and cut into
  wedges**
Fresh whole strawberries
Fresh pineapple, cubed
Small clusters of seedless grapes
Cantaloupe balls
Watermelon balls

glaze

1 cup sugar
**1 slice of ginger root to flavor the
  glaze**
¼ cup water

Prepare and attractively arrange the fruit on a lightly oiled serving dish. Bring the sugar, ginger, and water to a boil over high heat. Stir just until the sugar dissolves. Continue to boil the syrup until it reaches 300°F as determined by a candy thermometer. This is the hard-crack stage, when a small amount of syrup dropped into cold water immediately forms a hard, brittle thread. At once dribble the syrup over the arranged fruit to coat each piece as much as possible. The syrup quickly hardens to a crunchy, clear, sparkling glaze on the fruit. This is a delicious contrast to the soft fruit beneath.

almond cookies

Yield: About 3 dozen

1 cup hydrogenated shortening
1 cup sugar
1 egg
2 teaspoons almond extract
3 cups sifted all-purpose flour
3 dozen blanched whole almonds

Preheat the oven to 350°F. Cream together the shortening, sugar, egg, and almond extract. Stir in the flour 1 cup at a time. The dough will be very stiff. Form dough into round balls the size of small walnuts. Place on a greased baking sheet and flatten to form thick rounds. Press an almond into the center of each cookie. Bake for 10 minutes. Remove, and cool on a wire rack. Store in an airtight container.

mandarin fruit

Yield: 4 to 6 servings

2 11-ounce cans mandarin oranges
1 1-pound 4-ounce can lychees
 (available in Oriental-food
 stores)
1 tablespoon lemon juice
2 slices ginger root

Combine oranges and lychees with the syrup from both. Add lemon juice and the slices of ginger. Chill for a few hours before serving and remove slices of ginger root.

baked custard

Yield: 4 to 5 servings

2 cups milk
¼ cup honey (or ¼ cup sugar)
4 egg yolks (or 2 whole eggs)

⅛ teaspoon salt
1 teaspoon almond extract (or vanilla)

Blend together the milk, honey, salt, and egg yolks. (If yolks are used, the custard will be creamier in texture than if whole eggs are used.) Beat well. Add the almond extract and pour into custard cups. Place the custard cups in a baking pan with an inch of hot, not boiling, water. Bake at 350°F for 30 to 40 minutes, until firm or a knife inserted near the edge comes out clean. Do not overbake or the custard will separate and become watery and porous.

chinese almond torte

Yield: 6 servings

2 eggs
1½ cups sugar
¼ cup sifted all-purpose flour
2½ teaspoons baking powder
¼ teaspoon salt
2 teaspoons almond extract
½ cup slivered almonds
1 medium apple, finely chopped

Preheat oven to 350°F. Beat eggs until light. Gradually add sugar and beat until thick and lemon-colored. Sift together the flour, baking powder, and salt. Fold into the egg mixture. Add almond extract, nuts, and apple. Fold in gently. Pour into an 8-inch-square baking pan and bake for 25 minutes.

peach coupe with cherries jubilee

Yield: Approximately 6 servings

1 can (1 pound 14 ounce) pitted
**   black Bing cherries**
1 tablespoon sugar
1 tablespoon cornstarch
1 cup cherry juice
1 piece (3-inch) lemon peel
2 tablespoons cherry liqueur
6 canned cling peach halves
1 pint vanilla ice cream
⅓ cup warmed brandy

Drain cherries and reserve juice. Mix sugar with cornstarch and add 1 cup cherry juice a little at a time.

Add the lemon peel and cook gently, until clear and thickened, about 5 minutes. Remove from heat. Take out the lemon peel and stir in the cherry liqueur and the cherries. This may be prepared ahead.

To serve: Have the dessert dishes ready on a tray at the table. Place a peach half and some ice cream in each. Transfer the sauce to an electric wok and heat gently. Pour the warm brandy over the hot sauce, without stirring. Set ablaze and spoon over the peaches and ice cream.

index

A-B

Bass, Steamed Sea   73
Bean Sprouts, Stir-Fried   65
Beef
   and Pork with Bean Sprouts   22
   Chinese   132
   Cubes, Deep-Fried   101
   Deep-Fried, with Scallions   91
   Foil-Wrapped   121
   Fuji   26
   Ground, Oriental   132
   Red-Stewed   109
   Red-Stewed Shin of   108
   Shredded, with Vegetables   30
   Shreds with Carrots and Green Pepper   22
   Stroganoff   25
   Szechwan   55
   Tongue, Red-Stewed   109
   with Asparagus and Hoisin Sauce   15
   with Bamboo Shoots and Peppers   20
   with Bean Sprouts and Mushrooms   18
   with Celery and Celery Cabbage   19
   with Chow Mein Noodles   24
   with Oyster Sauce   20
   with Snow Pea Pods and Cashews   19
   with Snow Pea Pods and Mushrooms   18
   with Snow Pea Pods and Water Chestnuts   15
Broccoli, Stir-Fry, with Shoyu Ginger Sauce   64
Buns
   Deep-Fried Date   82
   Steamed Date   82

C

Carrots, Sweet-and-Sour   66
Celery and Mushrooms   67
Celery Cabbage, Steamed   75
Chicken
   and Shrimp with Vegetables   38
   Bits, Oriental   122
   Deep-Fried, with Lemon Sauce   90
   Javanese, Casserole   134
   Oriental, with Chinese Mushrooms   44
   Paper-Wrapped   103
   Pineapple, with Sweet-and-Sour Sauce   39
   Shredded, with Almonds   38
   Soy Sauce   110
   Stewed, with Pork   110
   Sweet-and-Sour, with Cucumbers and
     Cantaloupe   31
   Szechwan (Kang Pao Chicken)   56
   Wings with Oyster Sauce   35
   with Almonds and Mushrooms   46
   with Asparagus   33
   with Bean Sprouts and Snow Pea Pods   33
   with Celery and Celery Cabbage   36
   with Celery and Mushrooms   39
   with Green Pepper and Cashews   36
   with Green Peppers and Bamboo Shoots in
     Oyster Sauce   37
   with Hoisin Sauce   34
   with Mushrooms (Moo Goo Gai Pan)   34
   with Peas and Mushrooms   42
   with Sweet-and-Sour Tomato Sauce   42
   with Walnuts   35
Chinese
   Celery Cabbage, Stir-Fried   65
   Rolls   122
Cookies, Almond   140
Currant-Chutney Sauce   101
Curry Powder
   Less-Simple Version   79
   Simple Version   79
Curry Sauce   102
Custard, Baked   140

D

Dips, Hot-Pot   105
Dough
   Leavened   75
   Unleavened   75
Duck
   Peking   124
   Szechwan   54
Dumplings
   Cantonese Steamed Pork   78
   Indian Spiced Ground Beef   79
   Northern-Style Pork   81
   Vietnamese Fried   80

E

Egg Roll
   Filling, Pork   100
   Filling, Shrimp   98
   Wrappers   98
   Wrappers, Skillet   98
Egg Rolls   96
Eggs
   Foo Young   129
   with Bean Sprouts   129

F

Fish
   Deep-Fried, with Sweet-and-Sour Sauce   88
   Steamed, with Black Bean Sauce   72

Steamed, with Scallions and Ginger   72
Fruit Dessert, Spun-Sugar   139

G

Ginger-Soy Sauce   86,106
Green Beans
   Stir-Fried   63
   with Black Bean Sauce   63
   with Sweet-and-Sour Sauce   63
   with Water Chestnuts   63

H-J

Horseradish Sauce, Fluffy   102

Kebabs, Oriental Cocktail   136

L

Lamb, Chinese Style   133
Liver, Calves, with Bean Sprouts   29
Livers, Chicken, with Eggs and Noodles   43
Lobster Cantonese   62

M

Mandarin
   Combination   52
   Fruit   140
Meatballs
   Sari's Hong Kong   138
   Sweet-and-Sour Chinese   24
Mushrooms
   Chinese and Bamboo Shoots with Hoisin
     Sauce   64
   Stuffed   136
Mustard
   Cream Sauce   106
   Dip, Hot   105
   Sauce   79
   Sauce, Hot   86

N

Noodles, Fried   60

O

Omelette
   Mushroom   130
   Watercress   130
Oriental Firepot   107

P-Q

Pancake Rolls, Crispy, with Pork   100
Pancakes, Mandarin   128
Peach Coupe with Cherries Jubilee   141

Pearl Balls   74
Pork
   and Spring Onions   50
   Barbequed   135
   Curried, with Shrimp   50
   Deep-Fried, with Sweet-and-Sour Sauce   90
   Javanese Spiced   126
   Loin, Oriental   127
   Sesame, with Sweet-and-Sour
     Vegetables   93
   Shoulder, Red-Stewed   109
   Spicy Chunking   48
   Stew, Almond-Sprinkled   125
   Stew, Oriental   128
   Sweet-and-Sour   89
   Twice-Cooked Szechwan   56
   with Oyster Sauce   48
   with Peppers and Cashews   49

R

Radishes and Celery, Marinated   137
Rice
   Fried, Sub Gum   69
   Fried, with Chicken and Ham   68
   Fried, with Ham   70
Roasted Salt and Pepper   55
Roquefort Butter, Deviled   101

S

Sauce Diable   102
Scallops, Deep-Fried, with Sweet-and-Sour
   Sauce   92
Shrimp
   and Egg Fried Rice   68
   in Garlic Sauce   59
   Oriental   131
   Puffs   137
   Sweet-and-Sour   58
   with Bean Sprouts   60
   with Chicken and Cauliflower   58
   with Cucumber   60
   with Lobster Sauce   57
   with Mushrooms and Celery   62
Soup
   Bird's Nest   114
   Celery Cabbage and Pork   116
   Celery Cabbage and Shrimp   116
   Chicken   118
   Chicken Egg Drop   112
   Chinese   115
   Clam   112
   Corn and Chicken   113

Cucumber 117
Fig and Pork 120
Green Mustard Cabbage and Dried
    Shrimp 117
Hot-and-Sour 112
Imitation Bird's Nest or Long-Rice 114
Lotus Root and Pork 118
Noodle 119
Peking Egg Drop 111
Pork and Watercress 115
Spinach, with Pork 120
Watercress 118
Soy-Sesame Oil Dip 105
Spareribs
    Barbequed 47
    with Black Beans 74
Spinach, Tossed, with Peanuts 67
Spring Onion Flowers 47
Steak
    Green Pepper (Version 1) 14
    Green Pepper (Version 2) 14
Sub Gum ("Many Costly Things") 51
Sweet-and-Sour Dip 106
Sweet-and-Sour Sauce
    Pungent 106
    Richer Version 78
    Simple Version 78

T-U

Tempura Batter
    Beer 85
    Golden 85
    Light, Fluffy 85
    Thin and Crunchy 85
Tempura Dipping Sauces
    for Chicken 87
    for Seafood 86
    Ginger-Soy 86
    Hot Mustard 86
    Lemon 87
    Plum 87
Torte, Chinese Almond 141

V

Vegetable
    and Ham Rice Cake 70
    Medley, Sweet-and-Sour 66
Vegetables
    Crispy, Fried 99
    Five Precious Oriental 67
    Mixed, Chinese Style 69
    Oriental 44

W-Z

Water Chestnuts with Bacon 137
Won Ton Rolls, Adele's 121